# *from* Mrs. *to* Ms.

## A Guide to Living Your Life During and After Divorce

Melissa Nickelson

Passion Publishing

*from* MRS. *to* MS.

*A Guide to Living Your Life During and After Divorce*
by Melissa Nickelson

Published by Passion Publishing
5201 West Freeway, Suite 100, Fort Worth, TX 76107
www.FromMrsToMs.com
www.MelissaNickelson.com



Cover Design: The Kingfisher Group
Interior Design: Davis Creative, www.DavisCreative.com



Library of Congress Control Number: 2016948648

ISBN: 978-0692410639

2016

Printed in the U.S.A.

## In Praise of *From Mrs. to Ms.*

"All of us face crises in our lives but few as devastating as a divorce. If you are one of those life-long learners who see divorce as an opportunity to learn more about yourself and grow from your mistakes, this book is like a hand stretched out to lift you up and set you on the path to a new fresh life, one where you can be anything you want! Now, thanks to this book, you have the skills to find the real you within the shambles of a broken marriage, new strategies for developing greater self-awareness and self-care, and the confidence to move forward to a new fulfilling life. Best of all, learn how to walk through the darkest of your emotions and emerge into a clearing, where you are standing on your own two feet again and have become your own superhero."

-Dr. Jayne Gardner, Master Certified Coach
Author of *Divine Intelligence* and *How to Influence Other People*;
Owner of the Gardner Institute, a place for spiritual advancement

"This should be mandatory reading for every woman going though, or has been through, a divorce. This book will empower women going through one of the worst times of their lives. What a great guide for every woman to become the person they want to be."

-Cindy V. Tisdale, Fellow American Academy of Matrimonial Lawyers; Board Certified Family Law, Texas Board of Legal Specialization

"*From Mrs. To Ms.* Is a practical guide that comforts and inspires. Written in Melissa's personable voice, the reader will feel a warm hug from a dear and wise new friend!"

-Mimi Heines, Professional Certified Coach
Owner of Self Equity Coaching

"This book is a great resource for any client—Melissa gives practical, no nonsense advice in an easy read with heart! Not all clients have the time or the funds for a divorce coach, but every client will find something useful in this book."

-Wendy S. Burgower, Burgower & Rainwater, LLP
Board Certified Family Law, Texas Board of Legal Specialization

*This book is dedicated to women*
*who lost themselves,*
*got divorced, and battled their way*
*to a new life.*

# TABLE OF CONTENTS

# INTRODUCTION

Life has taken a turn, one you were not planning on. Divorce is not something you dream about as a child. When you were young and playing dress up, there was not a costume for divorce. You probably never daydreamed of getting a divorce one day.

In reality, divorce happens and can leave you feeling alone, depressed, unsure and an emotional wreck, among other emotions. This book is not going to focus on what went wrong in your marriage, or what your husband did wrong. It is only going to focus on you and the steps you need to take to move forward, leaving the divorce and all the emotional mess and baggage behind you. It takes time, patience, self-awareness, self-discovery, willingness and determination to move beyond the divorce.

This book is a guide to help you navigate the emotional side of divorce and start living YOUR life—a new life that can be anything you want it to be. You decide who you want to be moving forward and what your life is going to be like. Do not let the divorce define you. Learn from the mistakes and move on. Work through the emotions so you will not make the same mistakes again. Become a stronger person, learn new things, get involved in your community; anything to help you grow as a person. Start to live YOUR life, and make it a life filled with love, laughter, joy, peace, happiness and confidence.

This book will guide you through managing your emotions. It will help you discover who you are now and who you want to become. Then it will help you develop a plan to achieve those goals. This book is about helping you overcome the divorce, gain self-confidence, and start *living* YOUR life, not just surviving. Discovering who you are will help you move forward and free yourself from self-doubt. When you know who you are, you start making better choices, become more confident, and seek to live the life you want.

Examining your life after a divorce, or even while going through a divorce, is not easy. If you are in the middle of a divorce, you probably feel overwhelmed with all of the changes in your life. If your divorce is final, it is time to exhale and start building your new life. With your emotions and life in disarray, it is always good to seek guidance where you can.

I know firsthand the struggles and difficulties of starting over after getting divorced and jumping back into the job market. I went back to school, became a legal assistant, and worked in the area of family law. I have now experienced both sides of the divorce process. Throughout the years, I noticed that during and after a divorce, there is little-to-no guidance on how to put your life back together and deal with all of the emotional baggage.

This book grew from my desire and determination to help women handle the aftermath of divorce, to believe in themselves, and to offer guidance on how to live life again. The focus is on you and becoming aware of who you are, learning strategies for self-care and how to make peace with yourself. Gain confidence to move forward and live YOUR life. There are so many mixed emotions and feelings after a divorce, and the goal is to pick yourself up and move forward. I will provide you with tips and tools to help you discover your own talents and see yourself for who you are, a strong woman who has experienced a life-altering event. This book will help you let go, define your purpose, learn to become your own superhero, and motivate, activate and participate in your new life. I hope you are ready to look at yourself, put one foot in front of the other, hopefully in a cute pair of shoes, and dance your way through life.

It is time to let go of the past and start discovering who you are now. Chart a new life plan with changes to help propel you to become the best you can be.

# My Story

I was an emotional mess with a toddler in tow. My marriage had been dying a slow and painful death for a while, but I just did not want to become another divorce statistic and raise my son in a "broken" home. I stayed with my first husband until I was only a shell of the person I used to be and we were all miserable. There was not much joy or laughter anymore, even with a beautiful baby boy.

As we enter into relationships, we all bring emotional baggage, and I certainly had my fair share. My parents divorced when I was 6, and life got messy. I was raised by a single mother with three daughters, and my father was not very involved during most of my childhood. I never dealt with the emotional baggage of parents who could not get along, even for the sake of their daughters. It was traumatic and I didn't realize how much of their wounded actions I took on. I carried that family history into my first marriage.

I met my ex-husband, R, through a friend at work, and we immediately connected. We dated, had fun, and decided to get married, even though we had our ups and downs during the time we dated. Two weeks after the honeymoon, his mother, who was a wonderful, loving person, found out she was terminally ill with cancer and only had a few months to live. Devastation set in. We began a journey of trying to be with her as much as two people with full-time jobs could, all the while letting her spend her last remaining days at home. It was a struggle. She died right before Christmas, and our world collapsed. R was an only child whose father died of cancer when he was 12, and now his mother, his rock, had died.

Life was hard. R and I did what most young people do when they do not want to deal with the difficult emotions: we partied and drank. Life was not much fun at this point. Then one day I thought I was pregnant. It turned out to be a false positive, but from that point on, we wanted to have a baby. I wanted to give R a new family to love and, hopefully, hold our family together. After a brief separation, and a lot of guilt, R and I got back together, and I eventually got pregnant.

I became a stay-at-home mom and life seemed good for a while. However, those unresolved feelings and emotions we had never dealt with from the death of his mother haunted us. R continued to drink, and it was becoming a problem. He was the only one working outside the home, and he expected me to be a 1950's housewife, which I became. The more he expected me to do, the more I did. After all, he was the one working so hard to support our little family. An unhealthy pattern of guilt started about this time, and I developed a "less than" mindset, one that told me that I should just follow along and do what was expected of me because my life, my happiness, was less important. At some point, I became tired of living a lie—the lie you tell yourself that you have enough and to just sacrifice yourself for the good of your family. The lie that told me not to break up my little family because I was unhappy.

We started marriage counseling, and what a disaster that was. It got so bad that I would not talk during the sessions because R would then yell at me in the car on the way home about everything I said. I had lost myself, and I was tired of the struggle. After a year of this emotional upheaval and many arguments, I had finally had enough, and I left our house with our young son. We moved in with my mom, and I started the journey of finding myself and getting a job. This took some time, and throughout this journey, R and I attempted several times to reconcile. However, we never dealt with the hard, emotional baggage we carried and ultimately divorced.

The actual divorce took almost two years. During that time, there were many fights, disagreements and threats. It was not a pretty sight, and I often felt battle weary. Some days I felt so overwhelmed that I would say to myself, *if I just go home I could learn to just live, to survive.* Guilt was my constant companion because I felt like I was taking away R's only family. R was not making life easy, either. He would often try to make me feel guilty enough to come home, or he would try to bully me to get what he wanted.

I had supportive family and friends, who often sat me down and told me the hard truths, things I did not want to see, feel or hear. I grew stronger; I started counseling and was learning to stand on my own again. R and I eventually got divorced and after that day, not much really changed for a while. We were single, but we were still living the guilt-bully cycle of life. I learned since R wasn't addressing his own guilt and emotions, he was projecting them on to me. It was awful and took years for me to finally stop and not assume his guilt anymore. At some point, I realized that I could only control my own actions; I could not control or take on his. It was a time of self-discovery for me, as I learned to stand on my own and to not let others drag me down. I am not blaming R for this; I am assuming my responsibility in the divorce. He had his issues, and I had mine. I was tired of feeling "less than" and was ready to fight for myself and create a better life for our son and me.

Throughout all of the hard times, R and I co-parented our son together, which was not always easy. As the guilt-bully cycle reared its ugly head, I had to learn not to let it take over. I had to learn how to face whatever was happening rather than react to the emotions the situation evoked.

That is but one of the many emotional journeys of heartache, guilt, and shame that I lived through, but I can tell you once I learned to stand up for myself, and to be me, the stronger I became. If I can help shorten your learning curve, then please let me help you. You are not alone on this journey. Know there are people who care about you that will help you. Get out of your own way and ask for help. Do not let the powerful guilt-bully cycle hold you hostage; once you break free from its hold, you will learn to fly and become the best you can be.

Again, we all carry emotional baggage into relationships, and sometimes the weight of it all is just too much to bear. When you do not deal with the emotional baggage, it just keeps weighing you down until you almost break. It always seems easier to deal with someone else's baggage than our own. This is the hard side of learning to deal with your emotions. To enter into a new relationship, you must be open and honest. You must know your strengths and weaknesses, know who you are, and to not allow yourself or anyone else to take this away from you. You must be who you are and not lean on someone else to define you.

I will continue to share parts of my personal story throughout this book to both exemplify what I did and to offer tips on what you should not do. Hopefully, these stories will help you make better decisions.

I share my story with you so you know that I have experienced the emotional trauma of divorce, survived its aftermath and learned how to move forward and live life. I am aware of the day-to-day struggle, the emotional ups and downs and feelings of loss and loneliness. When I decided to work on myself and face the difficult emotions, I discovered I had the courage to change my life. I realized I had the strength and the power to live my own life and became a strong, independent woman. I stumbled, fell, picked myself up and learned a lot of things about myself and am now living an extraordinary life, full of blessings. You can, too.

SECTION I:

# DEVELOPING GREATER SELF-AWARENESS

## Chapter 1

# WHOSE LIFE IS THIS?

Do you feel as if you are truly living your life? Or do you just function and get by? What does it mean to really live your life? Do stress and constant worrying leave you feeling overwhelmed? Are you present in your life?

It is, after all, your life, and the question can either throw you off or make you stop and think. Are you aware and present in your life? Or, do you have your head down, putting one foot in front of the other, just going through the motions? Are you ready to leave the past behind and live in the present?

If your answer to the last question is yes, then it is time to figure out who you are, to become aware of your true self and your habits, thoughts, and life. To become aware of who you are, you must discover things about yourself. You must figure out what you want and how to get there. At times this journey can be painful as no one likes to acknowledge their mistakes or aspects of their lives that are embarrassing, hurtful, or wrong. We all make mistakes. The lesson is not to continually dwell on your mistakes, but to learn from them.

How do you learn from your mistakes? You must first become aware of the mistakes. It is hard to say your marriage was a mistake if it produced children, yet the mistake is what went wrong or what happened to the marriage. You need to take responsibility for your part in the breakup of the marriage and decide what you can do differently moving forward. You do not want to repeat the same mistakes in the future.

To become aware of your mistakes, you must first acknowledge the mistakes you made. Once you acknowledge the mistakes, you must become aware of when you are either making the mistake or about to make the mistake. It takes time and patience to change a pattern; do not give up. Become aware of when you usually make the mistake or act out. What elicits this behavior? How do you usually respond to this behavior? What can you do moving forward to not make this mistake again or act out?

Are you living a life that isn't really your own? Did you conform to society's standard of life? If so, you lost yourself along the way. It is time to discover who you are and what you want; it is time to live your life. The world hasn't stopped, have you? Are you moving forward or going backwards?

Do you want to change? Do you need to change? If and when you are ready to change, you first need to determine *what* you want to change, become aware of *when* you are doing what you want to modify, *what* triggers you to behave in a way you do not like, and plan *how* you are going to alter your behavior. Your plan needs to include how to stop yourself from doing what you want to change. For example, I knew I was drowning, becoming the victim of my own circumstance, and the only one who could change this was me. I became more intent on pleasing others than I was of taking care of myself. I became a shell of the person I used to be. When I decided to take action and start to stand up for myself, it was difficult at first as it caused a lot of friction. As a people pleaser, friction was difficult for me, yet I knew that I could not continue to ignore myself and my needs. I had to change myself and how I was handling things. I made a conscious effort to say what I needed to say and learn not to back down when something was important to me. I had to change the patterns of my own behavior.

Only you can change the patterns that hold you back, keep you down, and prevent you from moving forward and enjoying life. First, make a list of the things or behaviors you do not like and wish to change or modify. Be honest in your assessment. Determine what triggers this behavior and how you can become aware when an action sets off that trigger so you can modify your behavior or reaction.

If your plan is to change how you react to others or how to talk to certain people, your plan may be simply to stop and think before you speak, count to ten before you say anything, or to turn around and walk away, removing yourself from the situation. If someone provokes you and you know you are going to explode, you can either learn to avoid this person or learn to deal with your reaction to this person.

During the battle of divorce, you may need to reduce communication with your soon-to-be ex if all the two of you do is hurl accusations and insults at each other. The guilt-bully trip is unhealthy and must be avoided if at all possible; therefore, you must make a conscious decision to change and be very specific about what you want to change and the steps you are going to take to alter that behavior. Be realistic in the process, as it will not happen overnight, and at times you may revert to the behavior you want to change. If that happens, do not get discouraged. Talk yourself through the change you want to make, maybe reevaluate the steps to change and see if you need to make any adjustments, and start again.

Simple reminders of change are helpful. You see people wear a rubber band around their wrist as a constant reminder for something. Do whatever it takes to help you remember to change your behavior or habits. This is all up to you. You have to both want to change and have a detailed plan on how you are going to change, to actually modify your behavior or actions. I often suggest to clients to write down their thoughts and what they want to change in a journal. Make a list of the situations or actions that set off behavior you want to change. You have to be aware of the trigger that sets off the behavior. Becoming aware of the trigger will help you determine how you can change or respond differently. You can also make a list of how you want to change, the steps necessary to change, and see what steps work best for you. Break it down, make it simple to remember, and start taking the steps to change the behavior.

Also, make a list of the times you altered your actions so you would not do something you did not want to do. It is important to realize you have previously changed your actions, and you can do so again. Remember a time you reacted differently to something in the past that would have been a trigger for a bad reaction. What signaled you to stop that behavior? Can you use that same action to modify other actions? Only you can make that determination.

Becoming self-aware is both humbling and gratifying as not only will you identify things that need to change, but you will also become aware of the positive things and behaviors for which you do not give yourself credit. Start becoming aware of your actions and behaviors; you will learn a lot about yourself in the process.

I had a client who realized that every time he heard the special ringtone he had for his soon-to-be ex, he became anxious even before he picked up the phone. Just hearing that ringtone would set him up to do battle as he anticipated that she was going to be hard to deal with; he associated that ringtone with her and all of the emotional baggage they had together. He decided to change her ringtone to the general ringtone he used, and it changed how he reacted and responded to her. He no longer became anxious when she called. It is sometimes the small things that have the biggest impact. He made a conscious effort to change his behavior, and the first step was as simple as changing a ringtone.

There will always be challenges, problems and stress. If you are living from one stressful situation to another, it is time to eliminate as much stress as possible and learn to handle the stress so it does not run your life. I realize it is easier said than done, but it is a necessary step. A virtual spring cleaning of the clutter that holds you back is a good way to eliminate stress and things in your life you do not need or that hold you down. Part of improving your life is getting rid of situations, people and things that pull you down, waste time and energy or are needy. You are working through a lot in your own life; do not take on someone else's problems or issues right now. This is your time to focus on you and put yourself in a position to change what you want or need to change.

Only you can change yourself, and it has to start with you. You can stay a victim of your circumstances, be angry or sad forever, or take definitive steps to change your life. I have seen women who knew they needed to change, but they did not make the change because it would upset someone else, mainly their spouse. They decided to not change something because it was inconvenient for someone else, and they sacrificed themselves and their happiness in the process. Change is hard, and it often affects others; however, if this change is for the better, then only you can make that decision. Don't you want to be the best person you can be?

It is important to remember you can only change yourself and no one else. If someone does something that triggers you to act in a way you do not like, it is up to you to change. Even if you ask the person not to do or say that particular thing again, you cannot count on that person to alter their behavior. You are responsible for your behavior, so if change is to occur, it is up to you to change your actions or to not put yourself in a position that can trigger this behavior in you.

Change is difficult yet is constant in life. Usually change happens gradually over a period of time, and you are not aware of small, subtle changes. Then one day, you notice things are different. Self-awareness is seeing your actions and making the conscious effort to modify your actions.

**Tip:** First, make a list of the behaviors you want to change; be specific. Next, create a detailed, step-by-step plan on the actions you are going to take to change those behaviors.

*Chapter* 2

# Who Are You?

Who are you? Do you know who you are? Really, at this point in your life, do you know who you are? If you are getting a divorce, or are divorced, then almost everything in your life has changed.

After living with my husband and child in our marital home, it was difficult to move in with my Mom because in that household I was a child with a child. I was an adult living with my Mom who naturally wanted to take care of me. It took time to settle into a new routine, but we did. When I later moved out and on my own, I was solely responsible for my son and myself. I had to take care of everything, and at times it was difficult. However, it taught me that I can handle and take care of whatever happens. There were tough times, exhausting times and fun times. My son and I created new traditions. It was a time of transition, and it was during this time that I learned a lot about myself, and how strong I can be.

After a divorce, you may feel like you need a new identity, a new lifestyle and new habits. You are no longer part of a couple; you are single again and your life has drastically changed or is changing. You need to discover who you are as a person at this point in your life. Some people struggle with who they are after a divorce. You go from being someone's wife, a Mrs. to being a Ms.; you go from being one half of a couple to being alone. This is hard for some to comprehend and deal with. It can feel like the loss of an identity or worse. Yet, there are two halves to a couple and you made up one half, so maybe you only lost half of yourself.

Now is the time to figure out who you are, who you want to be, and where you are headed in life. Once you know this, you can decide if you want to make additional changes to yourself.

Let's start with who you are. Ask yourself the three questions below and answer them honestly. No one except you, unless you want to share your answers, will know how you answered these questions. We need to first establish a few ground rules for the following questions: (1) your answers cannot be *wife*, *mother*, *sister*, or *daughter*; and (2) the answers must be descriptive words about you, and who you think you are, right now, at this point in your life.

1. List five descriptive words that describe who you are:

   ______________________________________________

   ______________________________________________

   ______________________________________________

   ______________________________________________

   ______________________________________________

   ______________________________________________

   ______________________________________________

   ______________________________________________

This is a difficult exercise; it is hard to describe who you are especially if you are still emotional from the divorce. It can take a while to come up with five words, as no one wants to admit things that are unflattering. Reality is not often easy, and this exercise puts you, your actions and thoughts, up front and center. We are also our own worst critic and do not give ourselves enough credit for the good things we do.

Now, let's move on to the next question:

2. List five descriptive words that describe who you *want* to be:

________________________________________

________________________________________

________________________________________

________________________________________

________________________________________

This question requires you to think about the qualities you like and want to emulate. Look inside yourself, who do you want to be, and what characteristics do you want to have? I hope one of your answers is that you want to be happy and/or confident.

One last question: the answer can be one word, one sentence, one paragraph, or as long as you need it to be.

3. What stops you from being the person you want to be?

________________________________________

________________________________________

________________________________________

________________________________________

________________________________________

The most common answer I have encountered from what stops you is fear. Fear can stop you in your tracks; it can paralyze you and hold you hostage. I define fear as:

F – forward
E – energy
A – at
R – rest

Fear can stop you from moving forward, from putting one foot in front of the other. It can hold you in one place. Fear stops people from achieving their dreams, from doing something that maybe they have always wanted to do. How many times has fear held you back from doing something you really wanted to do, but were too scared to do? What meaning do you attach to your life when you are not functioning? What is your biggest fear?

Be honest with yourself when answering this question. Are you afraid of failing? Scared of looking dumb or embarrassed? Fearful of what other people will think? In reality, how many times have you failed? Looked dumb? Really cared what others thought of you—especially if what you are doing is helping you. Many times I hear people say that they did not want to tell anyone they were getting a divorce, or talk about the divorce, for fear of what others may think about them. My question for you is this: How many people do you know who are divorced? At any time during that person's divorce, did you or others gossip or judge that person? Probably not. You most likely felt compassion and wanted to help them.

We become so self-conscious of what we think other people are thinking or saying, we often do not see what other people actually see. When you are upset, you do not always think clearly and may become hypersensitive to what you assume others are thinking. This can become paralyzing and stop you from doing things or saying things, as you are fearful of what others will think. Fear can take over and control your life. Who is in control of your life right now: you, fear, society or someone else? Fear can and will stop you from moving forward. Do you resist moving forward into an unknown? Are you so afraid of change you would rather be stilted in life? What are you afraid of?

The anticipation that something is scary can build up in your mind and paralyze you in fear and doubt. How many times have you actually faced something you are truly afraid of that maybe is just a little irrational? How much time and energy did you expend on this fear? Or have you not done something because you thought it was too hard?

Again, the buildup in your mind may scare you into thinking you cannot achieve something. If you put the time and energy you used worrying or doubting into being productive, imagine what you can achieve! Is it hard? Maybe. The real question is: why would that stop you? How many times have you faced a difficult challenge in your life, worked hard and come through the challenge just fine? Probably more than you think. Remember those tests you studied for and worried you were going to fail in school? How many did you actually fail? Did your life end then? No, and it will not end now. Be your own cheerleader, build yourself up, face the challenges before you and start working, not worrying, on accomplishing what you want.

Keep in mind that fear also has a beneficial side. Fear can protect you from danger and prevent you from making big mistakes, as you might become aware of what you are doing or going to say that you stop and think before you take action. Be aware of the benefit of fear in the right sense, but realize it can stop you from living life and it limits your possibilities.

How do you become the person you want to be? First, it takes figuring out who you are right now, who you want to become, and the steps necessary to make the changes and to move forward with a plan. It takes a lot of self-examination and willingness to change. It will also take time. You will have some ups and downs, and at times think it is either not worth it or it is too hard. Change is hard. How many times have you heard this phrase? To change, you must want to change and set your mind to embrace change. To become the person you want to be, you will need to work at it daily and never give up.

If you still think you cannot change, then answer this question: are you the same person you were five years ago? Are you the same person you were last year? How about six months ago? The answer to all of these questions is no. The answer is no because you have changed, if only in small ways. However, some of the changes happened over a longer period of time, and you were not aware of the change, as it was gradual.

Have you ever stopped and asked yourself how you got to this point in your life? I mean, when you got married, life was great; you were so in love and never thought you would get divorced one day. Over time the relationship changed. Everything changes with time and will continue to change. Negative energy comes from people's unwillingness or inability to change or to accept change in life. What happens if you change nothing about yourself? Who does this hurt?

Let's focus on what you want or need to change about yourself and discover some things about you in the process. What change would be meaningful to you? There are many assessment tests and resources you can take to learn and discover things about yourself. (See the References and Resources page in the back of the book for a list of various assessment tests.)

Once you have taken some assessments, how can the information help you? It will give you insights you probably have not thought of or maybe do not recognize in yourself. Do you know your strengths? Do you need to know your strengths? Whether you are entering the job market for the first time or returning to it, it is important to know what you are good at so you can leverage these strengths. It is time to focus on your strengths rather than your struggles.

As children, we are taught to work on things and subjects in school that we did not perform well in. Emphasis was on improving our weakness, not on improving what we are naturally good at. I understand we all need to work and improve on what we are not good at, I just wish there was more emphasis on acknowledging what we are good at and building on those strengths.

If you are returning to the job market, stay positive and get creative with your strengths. Find a job or career you will both excel in and enjoy; do not just look for any job. When you feel useful, knowledgeable and are making a difference, your self-esteem and confidence will improve. You may even find yourself taking additional steps to improve and promote yourself. You will begin to feel comfortable in being you. Life will improve because you will have built a new life, one you created. What a good feeling to be able to take something devastating, learn from it, and turn things around in a more positive direction!

Life is what you make it. What do you want in life? How can you alter your behavior or actions to achieve your dreams? It is up to you to decide what kind of life you want and how you want to live it. Take time to look at yourself, and see if you want or need to modify things to enjoy life. What steps can you take to become happy and confident? Believe in yourself and know you are worthy of love, happiness and self-confidence.

Answer this question: To move forward, I need to:

______________________________________________

______________________________________________

______________________________________________

______________________________________________

______________________________________________

______________________________________________

Examples might be: stop feeling guilty for thinking of myself; learn to stand up for myself; stop being a victim and change my life; learn to love myself; learn to take care of my needs; stop putting myself last; listen to myself and trust myself, etc.

The flip side of not engaging in self-awareness is to live in denial or remain stuck in emotions which can leave you angry, hurt or not really living but simply surviving. That is not living; it is reliving the past and trying to make the outcome different. We have all made choices that at the time seemed easy but were not good for us long term. Acceptance of this is not always easy, but it is necessary to look at the big picture and decide what you want and need to change.

Time keeps moving forward. Are you?

**Tip:** What are you good at? What are your strengths? Know the importance of being aware of who you are, what you can do (accomplish) and do not let obstacles (fear) stop you. Life is changing, so advance with change; do not just roll with it. You are now responsible for yourself and your household. What changes do you need to make to take care of things? Make a list of at least three of your strengths and three changes you want to make in your life.

My top three strengths are:

1. ______________________________

   ______________________________

2. ______________________________

   ______________________________

3. ______________________________

   ______________________________

Three changes I want to make in my life in the next six months are:

1. ________________________________________
   ________________________________________
2. ________________________________________
   ________________________________________
3. ________________________________________
   ________________________________________

*Chapter* 3

# The Emotional Price Tag

What is the emotional price tag you paid during your divorce or the emotional cost since the divorce? Emotional price tag? What is that? During your life, you have made sacrifices and have done things you didn't want to do for the sake of getting along or compromising. During times of change or upheaval, when emotions are running high, compromise is hard to do. At times it feels like you just give and give and give and receive nothing in return. To move on you must pick your battles, stand your ground on what means the most to you, and let go of things you do not care about. This process takes a toll on you mentally, physically and emotionally. Thus, the emotional price tag is the price you pay to deal with high emotions and feelings. When you are hurt or angry, the emotional price tag is high. When the level of hurt is high, the emotional price is usually higher.

If you are tolerating your circumstances to stay where you are, both emotionally and physically, the trade-off may be too great. If the price is too high and wears you down, then it is time to change it. This is a good time to seek help. It is important to have a good team to support you, to hold you up, to guide and direct you when you need it the most.

Whom should your team consist of? Look to your family, close friends, people from your Church or other organizations, and a counselor, psychologist, psychiatrist or divorce coach. You will need help, so let those around you help you process all of your emotions. Surround yourself with people who will help you. This also means allowing people to be honest with you.

There will be times when it will be hard to hear the truth, but those close to you need to tell you the truth to help you move on. You also need to remember a lot of people will offer you advice, and that is exactly what it is—advice. You do not have to follow it. Realize they mean well and some may give you great advice. Stay true to yourself, but be receptive to their help as they offer their opinions or thoughts.

During the emotional roller coaster times, do not take your frustrations out on those close to you. They are there to help you, not to be your whipping post. If you hurt someone who is trying to help, apologize. It is never okay to hurt someone because you are in a bad mood or are going through a difficult time. Being upset does not give you a free pass to behave badly.

There is nothing worse than someone who constantly whines and never does anything to change their situation or move forward. This is how people run off friends during a divorce. Friends will help and support you, but at some point, they want you to start putting your life back together, to work on yourself, and to live life.

People have empathy and want to help, but if they feel like all you do is complain and do not do anything about it, then eventually they will no longer want to be around you. If you cannot move forward, it is time to seek professional help.

I have seen women who are so hurt they cannot move forward. They are stuck in "what if" or "how did this happen" and continually ask, "What if this never happened…" or "What if he changed….". Then there is the "if only" phase: "If only he would change" or "If only I wasn't so angry at him." You cannot live your life stuck in the "what if" or "if only" way of thinking. It is important to understand what went wrong; however, you may never fully grasp or understand what happened or what went wrong. Or you may be in denial as to what really happened or your role in what happened.

Remember, I didn't say this was going to be easy. I suggest you work on moving forward and not waste years worrying and crying about something you cannot change or have no control over. Remember the only person you have control over and can change is YOU. You cannot change anyone else. People change, good or bad, and you cannot change and go back to how life used to be. That life is no longer possible as it is the past. Time changes everything, and you must learn to adjust or the emotional price is high. The emotional price tag is hurtful and painful and you do not want to stay stuck in this phase, as it will take its toll on you and not allow you to move your life forward.

I worked with a client who was in the process of getting a divorce but did not want to get a divorce. Her husband had an addiction problem, and she, as his caretaker, enabled him to continue living with his addiction. He eventually moved out of the marital residence, and she discovered he had been seeing other women for a while. She was devastated, became depressed, and cried all of the time. She just wanted him to come home and kept saying, "If only he would stop seeing other women." During most of my sessions with her, she cried and wanted to figure out a way for him to come home. However, in between crying, she would tell me awful stories of how he had treated her throughout their marriage.

She just could not, and would not, accept that her marriage was over. She spent so much emotional energy on the "what if" and "if only" that she became paralyzed in fear and self-doubt. Yes, it is scary to radically change your life and get a divorce. Eventually, this woman pulled herself together, started to move forward, and rejoined the living and functioning world. She had to get past the block or the stigma of getting a divorce and not feeling like a failure. She didn't fail, her marriage did. Several things in her marriage were out of her control and, although she tried to control things, she could not. She is a lot happier now than she has been in a long time, and she will tell you that although she never planned on getting a divorce, once she accepted her marriage was over and got divorced, her life got better.

**Tip:** Manage your emotions, or they will run your life and not in a good, productive way. Seek guidance to help you deal with the emotional upheaval. You do not have to weather this transition alone.

*Chapter* 4

# LIVING A "DIVORCE LIFE"

What is living a "divorce life"?

When your entire life is consumed with the divorce and all you can think and/or talk about is your divorce. When everything in your life revolves around the divorce, it is all you can focus on. You talk to everyone around you about it constantly. It is the first thing you think about when you wake up and the last thing you think about before going to bed. You talk to anyone and everyone who will listen about the divorce and all the sordid details. You are like the Energizer Bunny®, always talking about the divorce and never stopping. This can become habit-forming and very destructive. Yes, divorce can become all-consuming if you let it.

If you are struggling with emotions and cannot get off the emotional roller coaster, please seek professional help. You must remember: life does go on. Yes, divorce is painful and hard, but you must move on. There is more to life than the divorce. The divorce is temporary, and although it may feel like it is going to last a lifetime, it will not—unless you let it.

How many people do you know, who during their divorce, were so caught up in the drama, hurt and anger, that they could not focus on anything else? When you saw them, did they only talk about themselves and their problems? Did they ever ask how you were doing?

Then there are the people who years after the divorce talk and act as if the divorce just happened. You then find out it was final 5 or 10 years ago. These people are reliving their divorce. They have either not moved beyond the anger and hurt, or they are in denial. They are stuck in the past and filled with resentment. It is difficult to be around people like this, as their personality is so negative, and it appears everything in their life is someone else's fault.

You do not want to be this person. If you see yourself in either of these scenarios, then please seek professional help as you are not living life; you are living a "divorce life." Yes, you may be getting a divorce, or have been divorced, but you still have a life. It is just a life with divorce in it.

If you are living a "divorce life", you will lose friends. People will start to avoid you and you may wonder why. At some point, people get tired of being around someone who is constantly living in the past. It is tiring to be around someone who is negative, whining or crying and not making strides to put them self together and live in the present. There is not a timeframe for when your friends say, "Enough," but you will sense it if you are paying attention. Remember, just because your life turned upside down is not a reason to be impolite and not ask how someone is. It is a good distraction to talk about someone else's life. Ask how their children or their parents are doing, anything to keep the conversation from venturing into only you and your life. Friends and family like to share, and part of sharing is caring about others and what is going on in their lives.

Staying locked in anger, constantly talking about your divorce, your ex-spouse, and everything that went wrong in your marriage is not moving forward. It is problematic when you do not work through the emotions and live out these feelings every day. It is living in the past, full of negative emotions, energy and a continually bad attitude. Living a "divorce life" is not healthy; it is toxic. Do not let the divorce take over and run your life. Is this who you want to be or to be known as? If your answer is no, take steps to change your outlook and attitude. Yes, life is difficult and the fallout from a divorce can leave you reeling and unsure. However, you are stronger than you think, so begin to take steps toward living a different life. Divorce is a process you are going through or have been through. Do not let it become your life.

**Tip:** How do you keep from letting the divorce take over and run your life? Here are some tips that can be helpful:

1. Seek the help of a professional, someone who specializes in divorce, who can help you manage the emotions running through your mind and running your life. Someone to hold you accountable, help you handle the issues and not stay stuck in the emotions and problems.

2. Have a select group of people, your inner circle, your emotional support team, and let them help you. People who will listen, offer advice and tell you the hard truths. Remember you do not have to follow their advice, but if you lean on them, they want to help and will offer words of wisdom and tell you what they think you should do. You need to have someone to "vent" to, so you can release the emotions.
3. Get into a new routine as soon as possible. You are now responsible for taking care of everything in your house whereas before maybe each spouse took care of certain tasks. Now is the time to establish new habits and a new daily routine. We are all creatures of habit although we do not like to admit it. The faster you get back into a routine, the less time you will have to worry about why things are not getting done and then feel overwhelmed.
4. Be aware of your emotions and feelings and how you react to others around you. Be mindful of how you treat yourself.
5. If you are still in the divorce process, work with your attorney to move the case along; do not let the case stall due to lack of work on your part. The sooner you are through with the process, the quicker you can start your new life.
6. Start working on something you want to change about yourself, whether it is starting a new exercise program or taking a class. You need to stay busy and not let your mind linger on the divorce. If you have too much time on your hands and nothing to do, then you might spend the time dwelling on the divorce and all the baggage it brings. This is not a healthy place to be.

SECTION II:

# STRATEGIES FOR SELF-CARE

*Chapter* 5

# Take Care of Yourself

Do you take good care of yourself? Do you take as good of care of yourself as you do your children or others? Taking care of yourself often seems selfish because, as women, we are normally the caregivers and take care of others. When did it become acceptable for women to put other's needs and wants ahead of their own and stop taking care of their own needs?

If you spend time caring for others and do not take time for yourself, you will lose yourself and your identity. You may feel guilty about taking care of yourself and putting your needs and wants ahead of others. Losing your identity is a dangerous road to go down; if you have already traveled down this road, it is time to reclaim yourself.

It is not selfish to take care of yourself; it is healthy. It is important you take care of yourself and make sure you are in shape both mentally and physically. How can you take care of others if you are not in good condition yourself? What are you teaching your children if you always take care of them first? That Mom always comes last? I am not saying ignore others to take care of yourself, I am saying you need to respect yourself enough to meet your needs and wants.

You are important and need to make sure you are taking as good of care of yourself as you take of others. During a divorce, when emotions run high, it is easy to put everything else before caring for yourself. If this happens, then depression can set in and take its toll on you. Often during a divorce you may lose your appetite, and weight seems to fall off. I call this the divorce diet. You are so upset you do not eat. You make look and be thinner, but your emotions are weighing heavy.

Let's work on all aspects of self-care: physical, emotional, psychological, and faith. You need to find balance in the midst of chaos. I will offer suggestions and ideas for each aspect and encourage you to incorporate these along with your own ideas to help care for yourself.

*Chapter* 6

# PHYSICAL HEALTH

At this point in your life, the thought of getting physical may either make you laugh or cry. I am not referring to being intimate with someone; I am talking about physically moving your body in exercise. During and after a divorce, you may be so physically exhausted that exercising is the absolute last thing on your mind. How are you supposed to exercise when you can barely get through a normal day? Not to mention sweating is not all that attractive…

However, not only is exercise good for you, it is also a great stress reliever. Imagine not only looking better, especially after that divorce diet, but also *feeling* better. If you are physically drained, how are you going to find the energy to exercise? I know it seems counterproductive, but moving your body will give you good, positive energy and will help clear your head. Find an exercise routine that works for you. Maybe running is not your thing, but how about walking or taking a dance class? Yoga, Pilates or ballet barre classes will certainly help you get into shape and help with mental clarity.

After some of these classes in the beginning, you may be too tired to feel any emotions. The only thing you will be feeling is muscles you forgot you had, living with the painful reminder of their neglect. This is the time to discover what exercise routine you like. You may try several before you find one that engages and works for you. Find one you like because, if you don't, you will soon lose interest and stop. Remember to start slow if you do not have a regular exercise routine. You do not want to injure yourself or burn out within the first few weeks; these are simple reminders we all need to remember. Once you start an exercise routine, it will make you feel better about yourself and boost your self-esteem.

There are also relaxing ways to care for yourself physically. Getting a massage, seeing an acupuncturist or chiropractor regularly will help you both physically and mentally. These may seem like an extravagance, but are relaxing and will help you more than you might think. You do not have to get weekly treatments to enjoy the benefits. Make it a monthly occurrence or as a special treat. This is all part of the plan to take care of yourself, so indulge when you can—YOU ARE WORTH IT.

Next comes diet, and I know that seems like a dirty word to some. I am talking about your overall diet, what you eat daily, not going on a diet to lose weight. Although the divorce diet will certainly help you drop weight, you still need nutrition to maintain energy and to be healthy. Diet affects you in many ways. Eating the wrong foods can and will affect your memory, body and how you function. You will need all the help you can get to start your new life, so take nutrition seriously. Find a good nutritionist or read all you can about nutrition and how food affects you. Food also affects your mental clarity, and it is important to care for your brain as well as your body. You can educate yourself on the proper foods to fuel your body, which will give you more energy to function day to day and to exercise.

Most people may not be aware of the importance of nutrition, but a body under stress is not good. Stress does horrible things to the body: it ages you (*and who wants that?*), causes disease, and breaks down your body, causing you pain and medical issues. The right diet will alleviate some of this and add to your overall health. Proper nutrition is vital to good health and part of you taking care of yourself. Do not neglect your diet. If you neglect your diet, your body will show the signs of poor nutrition. We all want to look our best, and it starts with diet and exercise. Learn to listen to your body; it will tell you what it needs or does not like. This is a big part of self-care, so take it seriously. You cannot return to good health unless you make diet and exercise part of a lifestyle change.

A woman I know learned she had cancer six months after her divorce was final. She was devastated, yet she had to keep going for her children. In between cancer treatments, fighting with her ex-husband, and taking care of her children, she was exhausted. She pushed through, started on a daily exercise program, and changed her diet. She looks amazing now and is cancer free.

Your physical environment also plays a part in your self-care routine. Where you live, where you work, and the places you go all impact your life, so surround yourself with places that are comforting to you. It is important to make the living environment *yours* and different from the marital environment. This is where you live, make it comfortable and decorate it to suit you. You are in control and can decorate it any way you want, without input from anyone, as this is now your domain. Paint the kitchen or den; redo the master bedroom. If you have children, tell them it is time to update and ask them to help. If they want to update their bedrooms, let them. This is about creating an environment that is about you, or you and your children. It is easier to walk into the family residence that you have made changes to than to walk into the residence that looks exactly as it did when you were married. Create a comforting space. You need to have a soothing place you can relax in. We all need a safe haven, and your living environment should be just that.

Now is also a good time to do something for you, something that you have always wanted to do. Get away. Take a vacation. Go on a cruise. Enjoy some down time. You deserve it and probably need it. Or learn something new; take a dance class, a pottery class, or any other endeavor you want. Go back to school. Do something to make you happy and show you can do things alone or invite a friend to join you. You have a new life now, so while you are making changes, indulge yourself a little. This is also part of taking care of *you*.

It is important to having something to look forward to, something you have planned and really want to do. It is also a sign you are feeling independent and ready to try and accomplish new things. Be adventuresome and do something for yourself. Do not be discouraged because you are single or someone else projects his or her dislike or fear onto you. You do not want or need negative energy around you at this point, so put some space and distance between those who bring you down.

**Tip:** Move your body, exercise, eat nutritionally, redecorate, be adventuresome and try new things.

Three things I can change immediately:

1. ______________________________

   ______________________________

2. ______________________________

   ______________________________

3. ______________________________

   ______________________________

Chapter 7

# EMOTIONS

During times of stress and turmoil, emotions can hit at any moment and sometimes the smallest thing can set off an avalanche of feelings. How do you get through the day when your emotions are running high and you are sad, mad or really upset? How do you get through the day without having a meltdown? How do you function without crying all afternoon? How do you pull yourself together and move forward rather than crawl into bed, pull the covers over your head and never come out? It is unrealistic and unhealthy to do so, as you cannot and should not remain in these hurtful emotions for hours or days, much less the rest of your life. On days you do not want to get out of bed, what would help you mentally and give you the desire to get out of bed?

We all experience times of extreme emotions, the kind where you want to go hide, yet at some point you must surface. Divorce is one of those times. A good cry really does help, as it can feel cleansing. If you are somewhere you cannot have a good cry, how do you hold it together? It is always good to talk it out with someone, a good friend, a confidante, family member or professional.

At times, you might want to tell the person you are talking to that you just need to get it out, to vent, and to please just listen and do not try and fix it. There are times a good cry and a good rant are all it takes to move past the emotions and get back on track. Other times, you may need more time to pull yourself together so you can make it through or function that day.

Let's talk about that kind of day. How do you get out of the emotional state and function like a normal person and not an emotional mess? First, I will tell you it is not always easy. Emotional pain is difficult and can wreck even the most upbeat, cheerful, positive person. For immediate results, distractions are always good. Go outside, change your environment, if only for a few minutes. Listen to an upbeat song but not one that will upset you or remind you of a different time. Fill up your calendar; do not give yourself too much time alone. You must take positive action, anything to take your mind off of your immediate feelings. (This is where ice cream or chocolate can come in handy.) Do anything to remove or distract yourself from the emotional divorce baggage, so you can function until you have time to work through the emotions.

Take it one step at a time, day to day. Be aware of your moods and your emotions and be cognizant of your thoughts. It is up to you to change your mindset. Determine what you want to change and what habits and thoughts you need to change. Do not let negative emotions and/or energy pull you down. *Fight for yourself; you are worth it.* Most of the time the biggest struggle is within you. You must stop the negative self-talk and self-doubt.

You must address these emotions, or they will forever stay with you. Therefore, when you have time to work through the emotions, a good cry or a good rant to your best friend are helpful. However, you still need to work on the source of your feelings. Where did the emotions come from, and why are they so strong? Is your emotional energy level drained? If so, you need to find a way to get it all out. Journaling is helpful, as you can write all of your emotions down, rant, get it all out. Just make sure you then destroy what you write. Do not hold onto it and remember—no one needs to read what you write, ever. A journal contains your private thoughts and emotions, whether temporary or permanent; it is a place for you to let it all out. This is not a one-time thing. You may need to journal daily to work through, get out and contend with your emotions. There are a lot of emotions, feelings, pain and anger to deal with.

Depending on how strong the emotions, you may need additional help in working through the feelings. This is where a good support system comes in: a counselor, divorce coach, pastor, or someone you trust to advise and help you. A good emotional support team is vital. Identify people you trust enough to help you work through the feelings and emotions, who can tell you hard truths—people you will listen to and will help you on your journey.

Just releasing the emotions will not eliminate the emotions. You must figure out where the feelings come from, get to the root of the problem. Work on how to deal with it, and then change it. Dig through your emotions; what issue keeps surfacing? Do you see a pattern emerging? You will need to work on these feelings, as there is a reason the same feelings keep coming up. Although it will be painful, you must acknowledge the difficult emotions to first understand then change them.

This is not fun. You will feel like you are on a roller coaster ride of emotions—up one minute, plunging down the next, and wanting to scream at the top of your lungs along the way. There are times you know exactly why you are upset, and other times, feelings of sadness or anger just hit. Divorce is hard, not only the business side of divorce, but the emotional side as well. There are times you are laughing one minute and crying the next. This is normal to experience, yet it's a good reason to work through the emotions, so you will not feel as if you are going crazy with your constant mood swings.

You hire an attorney to untangle the legal, business side of divorce. Have you hired a professional to help you untangle the emotional side of divorce? Many people think they cannot afford to hire someone to help them deal with their emotions or that they do not need help. Can you afford not to have someone help you address the various emotions you are experiencing? At times, you may feel as if the hard stuff is behind you, and then you plunge back into hurt, anger, resentment and disbelief. Your emotions are up and down and all over the place.

What is the emotional cost to stay in a constant state of upheaval? What does it cost you to repress the emotions, only to have them erupt like a volcano? It is not a pretty sight to erupt in front of others, which is usually when out- of-control emotions spew out of your mouth. You might feel better for a little while, then guilt usually sneaks in, and the vicious cycle repeats itself. You want to scream, "*Can someone please stop this emotional roller coaster? I want to get off!*" Are you beating yourself up because your marriage failed? *You* are not a failure; the marriage was. The marriage consisted of two people, who both need to take responsibility for it. Accept this and, although it can be tough, learn from it.

Find out what is causing you pain, and work through the emotions. Be honest with yourself. Be aware of your emotions and do not let them run your life. You must work through the emotions to move forward, and hiring a professional to help guide you is important. Divorce can and will trigger a lot of feelings that lead to soul searching and self-exploration. Your environment is or has changed and how you handle this will set the tone for how well you are adjusting.

Change is not easy; however, you can change. Remember, you can only change yourself and how you deal or respond to others. You must want to change for yourself and not someone else. It is important to understand you should only change what you want or need to change and not go against your values, morals or ethics to change for someone else or for the wrong reasons. Change because it will help you become a better, more confident person.

During a divorce, there will be a lot of times you might feel like just giving in, anything to get the divorce over with. I see people settle for things they should never have agreed to because they were tired of the divorce and the emotional roller coaster. Then within a year or two, they are so mad and want to undo the settlement because it is not fair or right.

I know several people who just gave up and forfeited a lot of assets because they were tired of fighting. I am not suggesting you continue to fight; however, to give up something that under the law you are legally entitled to and would receive if your case went trial is not always a good idea unless the fight and length of time it will take to resolve become too draining. I have seen men agree to outrageous payouts due to their own guilt and then cannot live up to the agreement, which then led to more issues and another Court battle, as well as another emotional battle. I have seen women just give up and walk away with nothing, stating that they did not need their husband's money and are better off without them. While this decision might feel empowering at the time, walking away from finances or other things that rightly belong to you and will help you re-establish yourself is not a wise decision. Know the law and what you are legally entitled to.

I personally walked away from some property and assets just to get the divorce over with, and within a year wished I had not walked away from certain things that had sentimental value to me. Pick your battles, and do not give up everything to just walk away *unless you truly feel it is best for you once you look at the big picture.* If you give in because you are tired of your soon-to-be ex bullying you, guess what—he will continue to bully you until he gets what he wants. If you have children together, he will most likely continue to bully you. This is why it is important to not make life-altering decisions when you are upset, emotional, and vulnerable.

Once time has passed and you become stronger and less emotional and feel capable of now contending with the division of the estate, if you have finalized the divorce, it is too late to negotiate a new settlement. After finalizing a case, most times the only thing you can change is possession or access of the children or child support and that requires another visit through the legal system. I am not saying you should stay and fight for everything; I am suggesting you not "throw in the towel" because you are tired of litigating.

Pick your battles, know where your boundaries are, *and do not let your emotions run the divorce.* That statement seems counter-intuitive, yet it is true. Do not let the roller coaster of emotions take over the business side of the divorce. This is why it is important to have professional help to address your emotions. If you are working through the hurt, anger, betrayal and other emotions, you are better equipped to deal with the business side of divorce. It is smart to be in a better frame of mind, and less emotional, when making important decisions which will affect the rest of your life. Do you really want to negotiate when you are an emotional mess?

It is not a good idea to make life-altering decisions when you are emotional. Think of a two-year-old who is upset and throws them self down on the ground crying because they cannot have something. This is how you may feel sometimes during the emotional trauma of divorce. Again, this is not a good time to make decisions that will affect the rest of your life. Therefore, it is smart to work through the emotions, so you can handle the business side of divorce in a rational, calm manner. Legal entanglements cause emotional distress and can certainly add to the feeling of being overwhelmed. This is why it is important to make sure you are in the right frame of mind when dealing with the divorce and making important decisions. Make sure you understand all that is happening each step of the way. Educate yourself on the legal system, and know what the laws are in your state on divorce. Knowledge is power, and making informed decisions will help you balance expectations and reality.

The key is to not only get the feelings out and address them, but to find out what method works best for you. What will help you deal with the emotions and move forward? Many times people try to deal with their emotions themselves and stay stuck in the same bad cycle. You do not want to make the same mistakes over and over. Yes, it is difficult to experience the emotions, as they are painful, but you must if you want to learn from this and move forward. It is time to contend with the emotions and begin a new journey in life.

I often hear people say they are working through their emotions, that everything is "in my mind and I am working on it." I always want to ask, "What happens when you cannot take the pressure anymore? Is your head going to explode?" There are times you might feel this way, with so much going through your head, as the emotions and the feelings are right below the surface, ready to pounce and take over. If you are just "handling" it by letting the emotions stay locked inside of you, then you are allowing your emotions to churn and hold you back. Time to vent, scream, yell, journal, write, talk to your emotional support team, your inner circle, a professional. Get it out, work through it, and let it go. The yelling and screaming are to be done either in private or with someone who is helping you. You do not want to have a full meltdown in public; people might think you are crazy. And although there may be times you feel you are going crazy, remember, it is a temporary feeling.

People are well meaning and may tell you how to handle the divorce or what you should do. Maybe a co-worker knows someone who got this or that in their divorce, and you should too. Understand what happened in their case may not happen in yours. People agree to things that may not apply or be an option in your case. Every case has its own unique facts. You need to hire an attorney who believes in you, works for you, but also will tell you the truth, not tell you something because you want to hear it. Divorce is hard enough, so make sure you are comfortable and confident in your attorney and they explain how the Court system works, how the Judge in your case usually rules, and what to expect.

You need to set boundaries, not only for yourself, but for others. It is important to not let friends and family steamroll you into something you do not want to do or need to do. This is your life, and you need to take control of it. People are well meaning and will offer you a lot of advice, and that is what it is: advice. Listen to what others say and use what they share if it will work for you. If not, you do not have to. Thank the person for their concern and advice, as it is their way of showing they care. Appreciate that others want to help anyway they can, but at the end of the day, this is your life and you decide what to do with it. You must live life your way. You are responsible for your actions and the consequences are yours and yours alone.

Negativity is contagious, so limit your access to negative people. Do not let them pull you down while you are building a new life for yourself. It may scare someone that you are courageous enough to seek a life you want, but that does not mean you need to continually hear how scary it will be. You already know it can and will be challenging. Do not let other people's fear hold you back. This is your life, not theirs.

**Tip:** Learn to manage your emotions, or they will manage you. Seek help to work through your emotions. Buy a journal or notebook to write down your thoughts and feelings.

*Chapter* 8

# EXPECTATION VS. REALITY

I often hear people say that once the divorce is over, their stress level will go down. They repeatedly say they just have to get past the divorce before they can focus on anything else. The reality is, once the divorce is over, a different stress or worry can set in. Beginning your new life journey can be stressful. Reality is often not anywhere close to our expectations.

How many times do you expect someone to act better, act differently or for things to turn out another way, only to realize it is not going to happen? It is the battle between what we expect and reality. It is worth repeating that you can only change yourself; you cannot change someone else. For example, if your ex-spouse was always rude to you, the divorce will not change his behavior. He will still be rude, and maybe more so, after the divorce. I frequently hear women say they thought that once the divorce was over, things between their ex-spouse and them would calm down and the two of them would become friends. Time for a reality check! Unless both of you have worked through your own emotions and are willing to change your behavior toward each other, most likely nothing will change except you are no longer husband and wife.

If you have children together, you must learn to co-parent your children and not let the old habits and emotions continue or get in the way. Unless both of you have worked on your emotions and attitudes, then behaviors will not change. You might expect him to change, but in reality, only he can change himself and his behavior, same as you.

It is important to know what to expect when dealing with the Court system and how a divorce can and will be handled. Perhaps your only glimpse of divorce was on TV and, honestly, that is not how cases are handled in real life. Maybe your knowledge of divorce is through a co-worker, family member or friend's case. As I have stated before, the facts in your case will differ from theirs, and you need to take all advice for what it is—advice. People mean well and want to help you, however at the end of the day, this is your life and you have to live with the results.

You may expect once a Judge hears your side of the story, you will get everything. That is not going to happen or very rarely happens. You must be realistic in your thinking and work with your attorney on obtaining the best outcome you can. You have to manage your expectations and live in reality. The reality is: you are getting a divorce, you will have to divide almost everything in your life, and you will get emotional. Be ready to handle those emotional days when they hit.

If you expect your ex-spouse, or soon to be ex, to be reasonable during or after the divorce, and he has never been reasonable, then you are setting yourself up for disappointment. *How your spouse acts or has acted will not change because you are getting a divorce or you are divorced.* Set your expectations to be realistic when dealing with your ex. You cannot change your ex, and he cannot change you. Again, just because you are divorced does not mean he will treat you better now. How he treated you before is how he will treat you in the future, unless he is working on changing. If he is angry and does not work through his emotions, then he may be more difficult to deal with.

Be realistic and set boundaries to protect yourself from getting hurt in the future. Boundaries are good when a relationship ends; it is like a barricade to shield you from intrusions. Healthy boundaries would include, for example: only talking with your ex regarding your children, and not continuing to hash out the divorce or marital problems. Do not put yourself in a position to always defend yourself and your actions. During and after a divorce, you are no longer tied to this person, unless you have children, and then you need to learn to effectively co-parent your children. This does not include telling them, or have them telling you, how to live your respective lives.

Old habits are hard to break, and although you do not trust your soon-to-be ex, it is easy to fall into the same pattern of bad behavior. I often hear clients say they just want to be "fair" and want their soon-to- be ex to be "fair." Reality is this: what is "fair" to you, may not be "fair" to someone else. We all have a different definition of what "fair" is, and it often is completely different than someone else's. I have heard women state that since their ex wanted the divorce, it is only "fair" that he continue to support them in the lifestyle they are accustomed to. The ex, on the other hand, might be willing to divide things in a more favorable manner until he hears that expectation. It may be an expectation a Court, by law, cannot Order, and then usually all "fairness" on his part is gone. Be reasonable and do not expect your soon-to-be ex to do or agree to something that may seem "fair" due to the circumstance but, in reality, is not.

**Tip:** Be realistic in your expectations. Manage your expectations, or reality will manage them for you.

Set three realistic boundaries for yourself:

1. ______________________________

   ______________________________

2. ______________________________

   ______________________________

3. ______________________________

   ______________________________

*Chapter* 9

# FEELING ALONE

I often ask clients what the loneliest feeling is, and usually the answer is sleeping in bed alone. This is the time they feel truly alone. In my opinion, the loneliest feeling is lying next to someone and feeling alone. To have someone right next to you, who either cannot or will not talk to you, is truly the loneliest feeling. I would rather be alone, by myself, than feel alone with someone lying next to me.

During times of loneliness, it is easy to tell yourself that others do not care or have time for you. If you are lonely and keep people away, you are setting yourself up for isolation. This can then lead to a path of not believing in yourself and thinking no one cares about you or that you are not worthy of love and friendship. Therefore, it is important to not isolate yourself, especially during difficult times. When you are lonely, reach out to others, tell them you need to talk or be around others. People cannot read your mind, so tell your friends and family when you are lonely and let them help you.

How do you combat not feeling alone or lonely, especially if you are not used to being alone? Time will help this feeling dissipate, and at some point, you may find you love your alone time. In the interim, plan outings with family and friends, connect with other single people and have a weekly dinner or meet after work. Seriously, fill your evenings up with events. This will reduce the amount of time you are alone. Clients tell me going home to an empty house is one of the hardest and loneliest feelings. As I mentioned in chapter 6, I suggest they decorate their house or apartment with things to comfort them. Surround yourself with personal things and things you love, so you will feel comfort in your surroundings. It is hard to walk into a home with bare walls and stark surroundings, so make it yours, even if it is only temporary. Hang pictures, display your things, redecorate, anything to feel comfortable in your surroundings. Get into a new routine as soon as possible. We are all creatures of habit, and starting a new routine, one that fits your life right now, is important.

If you have children living with you, it may be hard to plan outings with others, especially during the week. Your lonely time may be at bed time when the children are asleep and there you are, feeling alone. How do you get past this? What can you do? I suggest finding something to take your mind off of yourself and the situation. This can be the time you catch up on a TV series you want to watch, or read the books you have piled up since you now have the time. Reach out to friends you have lost contact with as you now have the time to devote to these friendships. Finding your childhood friends is easy these days with social media.

Taking an online course will occupy your mind and you will have less time to feel alone. Cuddling up to homework at night will help as you will not be focusing on being lonely, rather, you will be wondering how you are supposed to read five chapters of a book that puts you to sleep before the next assignment is due. There is no time for lonely when you fall asleep reading a textbook.

Answer emails, pay bills, journal; do anything to help you occupy your time and feel less alone. This is the time only you can decide or know what helps you. It may take a while to find what works for you, but do not give up. Keep trying until you find what you want to do, what makes you feel less lonely.

I will caution you to not fall prey to connecting with someone, a possible date, just to have someone to talk to. Times of stress and loneliness can make you a target. You might want someone to talk to and may lower your standards of what is acceptable behavior in a possible companion. During this time, it is best to connect with friends and family who know you and will be available for you. This is not the time to start dating. You need to feel confident and capable of being open, honest and emotionally available before you start dating.

This is also a great time to journal and work through your emotions and feelings. You have the time, and you are feeling lonely and maybe a little vulnerable. Use this time to work on your feelings. You can learn a lot about yourself during this period, so use the time to be productive and explore who you are. Journaling during the dark, lonely times is helpful to get the emotions out of your head, to stop the swirling of your mind. Get it out, and let it go.

Animals make great companions and are always ready for attention and to be loved and love you. They are always excited to see you when you come home and are available to spend as much time with you as you allow. Consider adopting a shelter animal. They need to feel love, need a home, and are great companions. Animals can take up a lot of time, depending on the animal. It will give you something to take care of, yet offer you so much in return. Plus, they are always available to sleep on your bed, if you let them. No more sleeping alone.

Another option for battling the empty bed syndrome is to put a large pillow in the middle of the bed. You will not feel so alone with half of the bed taken up. You can also sleep in the middle of the bed and take up as much room as you want. Oh—and hog all of the covers!

**Tip:** Do what you can to minimize the lonely times. Spend time with friends and family to fill up the lonely times. Do not let yourself sink down into depression.

One thing I can do to feel less alone is:

________________________________________

________________________________________

________________________________________

________________________________________

________________________________________

*Chapter* 10

# ATTITUDE

Do you know or remember the song *New Attitude*, sung by Patti LeBelle[1]? Below is an excerpt from the song, and the lyrics just hit home:

*Runnin' hot, runnin' cold*
*I was runnin' into overload, it was extreme*
*I took it so high, so low*
*So low, there was nowhere to go like a bad dream*

*Somehow the wires uncrossed, my tables were turned*
*Never knew I had such a lesson to learn*

*I'm feelin' good from my head to my shoes*
*Know where I'm goin' and I know what to do*
*I tidied it up my point of view*
*I got a new attitude!*

These words pretty much sum up how far emotions and feelings can swing during a divorce. Once you work on your point of view, you will have a new attitude. (This song is now in my mind and I keep singing it out loud. How about you?)

Many times during a divorce, your attitude becomes negative and you may feel all is lost. Is all lost? No, but an important part of your life is coming to an end. Life will go on, with or without you. Time does not stop, and thank goodness. You would not want time to stop and be stuck in the hurt, angry, sad, alone feelings divorce causes. Time does help and, in time, you will start a new life with new beginnings and possibilities.

I have clients cry, "But I don't want a new life! I want the one I had!" Well, if your spouse decides he wants a divorce, you do not have a choice. Life as you knew it to be is not an option anymore. You cannot turn back the clock to a better time in your life; you have right now and the future. If you live in the past, you are trying to recreate a different outcome for something that has already happened. You cannot move forward if you are stuck living in the past. Change your attitude; change your life. This sounds harsh, but it is a hard truth, and the truth is not always pretty, or easy, to accept.

Your attitude plays a big part in how you move forward. It is hard to put on a happy face when you do not feel like it or feel as if you could cry at any time. This is why grieving for the life you thought you would always have is important. The difference between the death of a spouse and the death of a marriage is this: after the death of a marriage, your ex-spouse is still alive and you may still see and have to interact with him/her if you have children. The similarity between death and a divorce is this: both are final, so take time to grieve and process the emotions.

After a divorce, you will change so many things that it can feel overwhelming. It can be difficult to have a happy, positive attitude, especially during the rebuilding of your life phase. However, you can accept what is happening or has happened, learn from it and move on, or you can let it take over and run your life. If you are living a "divorce life," then your attitude is not going to change. You are stuck in the down, sad, mad, angry world, or maybe you are stuck in the "poor me" phase. The "poor me" phase is when you blame everything on someone else, tell everyone how wronged you were, how no one loves you, and at some point, it may come true. You will run off your friends if you do not move out of this phase.

There are many phases of the healing process and, as hard as it is, you must go through them and work to move forward. Getting stuck in the emotional divorce baggage is not going to move you forward as a person. This is the time to work through the hard times and feelings, and make sure your attitude is aligned with how you want to be moving forward.

This is when you may have to really focus on something positive to change your attitude. Be grateful for the blessings in your life. Surround yourself with positive people, as a good mood is contagious. You will not always be happy, but moving forward with a good attitude, as much as possible, will help you. How many times have you heard the expression, *attitude is everything*? Your attitude says a lot about how you feel and where you are in life. Try to focus on the positive, be grateful, and let your attitude reflect that.

**Tip:** Life is better and easier to handle when you have a positive attitude. Remember: change your attitude, change your life.

# Chapter 11

# PERSPECTIVE

What is your perspective on life? Your perspective on divorce? What is your perspective on how you are going to change your life? How can knowing the answers to these questions help you? It can help you look beyond what is happening right now and see the big picture. Does your perspective change if you know circumstances will be different in a few days or a few months?

Maybe it will. Part of looking at the big picture is to see it from someone else's point of view. Look outside yourself and your emotions, and see how others view the situation.

Divorce can certainly change your perspective on love, marriage, and what is fair and right. It is hard to look at another person's perspective when you are at odds with each other. Does it help to see his point of view? Maybe he wants to see the children more, and you do not want him to. Think about how you would feel if you only got to see your children every other weekend? Would you be happy with this?

This is where you have to look past your own hurt and anger and do what is best for your children. Do your children want to see their dad more? While it may be difficult to be away from your children, you will have some downtime to do something for yourself when he has the children. Time to call the spa! Time at the spa can definitely change your perspective.

It is good to see both or all sides of the divorce, to understand where things stand, where emotions are and how to look beyond to get things settled. If you view the divorce from someone in your emotional support team's eyes, what do you see? Look at the divorce, or your life after the divorce, see the big picture, not just one or two issues. Does this change your perspective? Remember, life is constantly changing. Some changes are good; some are not. You have to be able to accept certain things in life, even if you do not like them. Divorce certainly falls into this category.

When dealing with other people's attitude and perspective, you need to understand their point of view or take into account their actions. This is also helpful when dealing with how others respond to you, and what you are going through. Some people will immediately start to wonder how your divorce will affect them. This seems odd, yet remember some people look out for themselves first and wonder how your relationship with them might change.

The aftermath of a divorce can leave some friends picking sides or choosing who they are going to remain friends with. Some people feel they have to pick a side to maintain a friendship or loyalty to one party. If this is the case, cut them loose and do not look back. You may not understand their perspective or like their perspective or actions, but you cannot change someone else. During a divorce, your perspective on many things will change and you need to be open to change and not let it paralyze you, leaving you stuck in one place.

**Tip:** Look at the big picture; it will help you make better decisions. Focus on what is really important, and do not get caught up in the little details that really do not mean much to you.

The most important thing in my life right now is:

_______________________________________________

_______________________________________________

_______________________________________________

_______________________________________________

_______________________________________________

_______________________________________________

_______________________________________________

*Chapter* 12

# GRATITUDE

Have an attitude of gratitude! It is hard to be grateful when you are an emotional mess or dealing with the aftermath of a divorce. You may be asking yourself if you are supposed to be grateful for the divorce, you are the only one who can answer this. I want you to focus on what you are grateful for. Are you grateful you woke up this morning? Being grateful you have a roof over your head, food to eat, and clothes to wear come immediately to mind. There is always something to be grateful for, always. Some days the gratitude might be that you survived the divorce. It is hard to be grateful when your life has been turned upside down, yet what lessons did you learn from this experience? This is not about always looking on the bright side. It is about seeing something good, even in the midst of adversity. It is about not allowing the negative emotions and energy to pull you down into the pit of depression and/or anxiety.

Research has shown being grateful can change your life as well as your attitude. It also shows people who are grateful experience less aches and pains and improved psychological health.

Being grateful can reduce negative emotions that are toxic to your health and wellbeing. Gratitude has the power to change your perspective. It is up to you to incorporate gratitude into your life.

Being grateful during difficult times helps you focus on the good things in life and not concentrate on all of the bad or difficult things. It will prevent your perspective from becoming jaded and taking things for granted. During the good, happy times, being grateful is easy, yet during times of stress and difficulty, we need to remember to live in gratitude for the good things in our life. It will help reframe your perspective and attitude.

**Tip:** Being grateful is good for your health and well-being. Living in gratitude can help you to not take things for granted, and it can change your perspective. With this in mind, make a daily list of at least three things for which you are grateful. During difficult times, you may need to list a few more things to change your attitude to one of gratefulness. And remember: there is always something to be grateful for.

List three things you are grateful for right now:

________________________________________

________________________________________

________________________________________

Chapter 13

# Psychological Health

Are you your own worst enemy or are you a friend to yourself? Are you beating yourself up mentally? If so, working with a professional during and after a divorce will help you make the transition from running on emotions to building a new life for yourself. A counselor, divorce coach, and/or minister or clergy will work with you, help you manage the emotional roller coaster you are on, and take steps to move forward. They will help you face the difficult times, deal with your emotions, and guide you through the process to start building your new life. It needs to be someone you trust who will hold you accountable as you work through difficulties and will stay with you through both the good times and bad. Getting emotions out of your head is good, yet you need to do it in a healthy way.

As I mentioned earlier, I frequently recommend journaling to my clients. It is a good way to release your emotions, good and bad, a way to express yourself and not worry about the consequences. This is the perfect place to vent your private, innermost thoughts and emotions. Write about anything and everything you are feeling and thinking. Write it all down. Get it out of your head. You do not have to monitor what you say, or how you say it, when journaling; just get it out.

When journaling, some thoughts or feelings linger and you may feel as if you write about the same topic every day. It will take time to work through your emotions, so be patient. Writing the issues out is good therapy and healthy, but it is not how things get resolved. It is through acknowledging the emotions, discovering what triggered the feeling, and learning how to change your response. This will direct you to the path of releasing the feeling. If you are continuously writing about the same thing, you may be rehashing a mood or thought. Feelings can linger and take over. If this happens, you can get stalled. Wait, isn't the purpose of journaling to get it out and move on? Yes. However, be aware that fear can add a new twist and keep you stuck. If you begin to over-analyze and cannot let an issue go, it is time to seek professional help.

I suggest to clients to write down thoughts either first thing in the morning before you get out of bed, before you go to sleep and your mind is drifting, or during a dark period. A dark period is when your mind is out of control and dark thoughts take over.

Journaling every day can help get your feelings out. When you hold feelings in, they build up. Eventually you will explode, and it will all come tumbling out. This is not a pretty sight to see, as it is usually done in anger, and ugly words come out.

Make sure you store your journal somewhere no one can find it and read it. No one should ever read your journal as it is a private place for your private thoughts. Do not let anyone read your journal—ever.

Once you have written it all down, shred it, burn it, or rip it up. I caution you not to keep your journal or read it later. The purpose of the journal is to get it out and move on, not to reread it later and continue to dwell on what you wrote.

If you have a hard time journaling, then try writing a letter to a person you are mad at. However, do not give the person the letter. This is another way to release the emotions and prevent them from building up. Do not stay in the dark period any longer than you have to. Get it out and move on.

You may discover after a while, when journaling, that your handwriting has changed. This can happen when you are changing an attitude about something. Maybe you are finally releasing it, and after a while, you will recognize what you wrote earlier in the journaling session is not as bad as you thought it to be. Maybe you made a bigger deal out of something, or were worried over something that did not happen. If so, you have switched from the emotional to the logical side of your brain.

Journaling can improve your health, as you are not holding in negative feelings and emotions. When you are on the emotional roller coaster, it affects all aspects of your life. When you have an outlet for releasing these feelings and emotions, you will feel better, both mentally and physically.

One of the benefits of journaling is writing engages the left side of your brain, the logical, analytical and rational side of the brain. Therefore, it leaves your right brain, the creative, emotional side of the brain, available to feel, to let out your emotions. Writing can help you see and then remove mental blocks, so you can release the negative and embrace the positive.

When journaling, use the time to not only address your feelings and thoughts but to also dream and plan. Write out goals for yourself, and see where the mood takes you. Journaling is expressing yourself through the good, the bad and the ugly. At the end of each journal entry, end the entry with something positive: your favorite quote, a prayer, a Bible verse, or something good that happened that day. You want to leave the emotions in the journal and focus on something good to move you onward. If you have a favorite saying or mantra, then write it at the end—anything to change your attitude, perspective and thoughts. This is a great time to list three things you are grateful for as recommended in the previous chapter. Some days, just getting the bad, negative emotions out is something to be grateful for. Other days, you may be grateful you survived the day. Anything positive, big or small, will help shift your mindset. List whatever you can, and you will start becoming aware of the good things in your life. It is good to turn to positive emotions before you move on with your day or evening.

**Tip:** Journaling is a good way to get emotions out, discover what is bothering you and work through it. Get the emotions out of your head and onto paper. It can release feelings of being overwhelmed, and it is a good way to let out and let go of your negative emotions. Be grateful for the little things in life—they add up once you become aware of them.

**Suggestion:** Dr. James Pennebaker has done extensive research on writing and journaling. I recommend reading his books and articles.

## Chapter 14

# FAITH

During times of stress or uncertainty, turn to your faith to help you through difficult times. Divorce is stressful and you will be faced with so many emotions, conflicts and unknowns. How do you get through each day? It is comforting to know faith will see you through this situation. Trust your faith, rely on your faith for help and guidance. You are never truly alone, look toward your faith for comfort.

Prayer is important and can see you through hard times and good times. It is good to pray and ask for help, guidance and direction, as well as how to handle certain situations. It will certainly help get your emotions out. You can pray anytime, anywhere and no one else has to know what and when you pray, or even what you are praying for. Prayer has a calming effect and can help you deal with immediate emotions.

Live in your faith, your truth, your beliefs. Know what you believe is important to you and how you live your life. Divorce may go against what you believe, and it can be hard to accept that you are doing something your faith does not agree with. If your faith does not agree or believe in divorce, it does not mean they are not accepting of divorce. Talk with your pastor, minister, priest, clergy or rabbi, and let them help you work through how this affects you and your faith.

Hope is a word we should all hold onto. At a Church conference I attended, the speaker said her definition of hope is: Help One Person Every day. There are days that person needs to be *you*. Help yourself on days you need it. This is all in line with taking care of yourself. There are several definitions of hope, and they are all meaningful. Find one that works for you, and let it help you. Be hopeful every day, hopeful things will get better, and you will move forward. Hope for another day, and another chance to live your life. Hope for a day filled with gratitude, joy and happiness. Hope you can help someone else in need.

**Tip:** Faith, prayer, truth and hope will see you through every minute of your life. Remember, you are never alone in this journey.

SECTION III:

# MAKING PEACE WITH YOURSELF

Chapter 15

# LETTING GO

After the divorce is final, things start to settle down. You are in a new routine, and it is time to make peace with yourself and your life. If you are still harboring anger and resentment, you have not completely worked through all your emotions. At times these feelings will surface, but if you are still frequently living under these emotions, you are not ready to make peace with the past and move forward. This is an important step, as once you let go of the past and all the hurt, anger, disappointment and any other feelings you experienced, you are truly ready to move forward.

It is vital to your existence to let go of all these negative emotions, to accept yourself, and to define your purpose. Even if the divorce was not what you wanted, it is done and time to look forward and not backward. It is time to begin a new chapter in your life, to get a fresh start. If you are reliving the past or trying to make the outcome different, work with a professional to help you break free. You cannot change the past, nor should you continue to live in the past. Live in the present and look forward to the future.

Are you putting all of your energy in holding onto anger, resentment or hurt? Are you holding on to a life you no longer have? All of the negative emotions and feelings need to go away, as you cannot hold onto them and move into a new life. If you do, you are still tied to a past that is hurtful and you are not ready to start a new life. It can be difficult to let go, as there were happy times as well as sad times. Hold onto the happy times; just do not let the happy times get weighed down by the sad times. Remember the good times, the happy times as good memories.

For example, you may still be living in the "what ifs": "What if he realizes he misses me and we can go back to the way we were?" If you are, do you want to spend the rest of your life regretting things you didn't do, or didn't do right? You cannot be sure things would have turned out differently if that one time you had done something different. Do you believe it would have changed the outcome? It is easy to look back and see mistakes and where you could have or should have done something differently. What is not easy is letting go and moving on.

If you let it, one thing can haunt you and hold you back from living your life. At this point, too much has changed and things will never be like you want or expect them to be again. Maybe you could work out some sort of truce. However, unless both of you are willing to work on the relationship and get past everything that occurred to end the relationship, then the same thing could happen again. Communication is one of the keys to a healthy relationship and at some point, the communication in your marriage broke down. This is how you ended up divorced and starting a new life. Time to let go of the emotions associated with the breakup of your relationship and move forward.

The divorce may be over, but you and your life are not. You have a life to live. Letting go does not mean erasing the past; it means you are not letting the past define you. Is the need for security holding you hostage? Do you turn to fear or security before you turn to being courageous? Is holding onto the emotions of the divorce providing you with a sense of security although it is a false sense of security? Knowing what you know now, would you go back to a broken marriage for a sense of security? If you are divorced, there were problems in the marriage; therefore, going back to the marriage would essentially mean living in denial. The pain associated with separation and divorce is hard and quite painful. There was pain at the end of the marriage and there was pain during the divorce. Hopefully, you are taking steps to move past the pain and into your new life. It can be scary to feel alone, yet going or staying in a bad relationship is painful, lonely and can deteriorate your self-esteem. Time to work through the pain and envision a new life for yourself, without the pain, anger, resentment and challenges associated with an unhappy life.

I call the trauma and the roller coaster of emotions during a divorce, "drama trauma", as many times this is what it feels like. When emotions are running your life, and everything feels like either trauma or drama, therefore, "drama trauma."

Then there is: everything is dramatic and must happen right now, this very minute, or it is traumatic! Problems or incidents are treated like the world will end right now if this does not get taken care of. For example: This is often when threats are being made—

"if you do not do ______________ right now, I am going to call my attorney." Someone is being demanding and wanting their way or else. That is not a good, or healthy, way to live.

I worked with a client who was constantly analyzing everything her soon-to-be ex said, emailed or texted her. She was trying to determine if there was a hidden meaning in what he said. She was struggling with the divorce, and every time he communicated with her, she was frantic. Replying to him was very traumatic for her, and she stressed over every response for a long time. Even something as simple as confirming pick up of their child became almost more than she could, or rather, would deal with. She was stuck in a cycle of bad drama and it led her to be traumatized about little things. This is not a healthy way to live. I often told her it was time to let go of the "drama trauma" and settle into a more relaxed way of living.

Living in "drama trauma" is letting emotions run your life and another way for your ex to continue to control your life. You are not married to this person anymore, and you need to break free of the cycle or habits binding you to him and the way you react to him. Stop worrying about what he thinks of you. You are not married to him anymore and need to learn to stand on your own two feet. Do not let his judgment of you get in the way of how you live your life.

The only difference between the "drama trauma" life and the "divorce life" is that in a "drama trauma" life, you are still complaining about your ex-spouse, but in a very dramatic way. It is stirring up incidents and creating theatrics that traumatize those involved, including your friends, family, those who help you, and yourself. You are compiling his faults and actions into acts of drama. You are still complaining and reliving your divorce and letting perceived faults or actions run your life. You are living with his presence, front and center, in your life. He is still influencing your life although you like to think he isn't.

If you are still caught up in his presence, what he does and says, what he thinks and how he treats you, you have not let go. This is different than talking to him about your children. If you have children together, you have to communicate and co-parent the children. I am talking about you not letting go of your relationship with him and, although you may be divorced, he is still a big part of your life in a negative way. Yes, it is hard to communicate and co-parent your children when the divorce is still fresh, but it is necessary. If you are acting like you are still married and worried about what he thinks or will say, you have not moved on. Part of moving on is letting go of the negative emotions and strings that tie you to your past.

Part of letting go is forgiveness, of oneself and others. You do not have to forgive someone because they ask for forgiveness. You need to forgive so you are not holding onto hurt, anger and resentment. In the end, if you are harboring these negative emotions, it will only hurt you. Forgive yourself and stop beating yourself up for things you have done wrong. Learn from your mistakes and move on. You learn the most when you stumble or make mistakes. Turn them into life lessons and change your behavior to reflect the changes. Forgiveness is necessary to letting go of what holds you back, what causes you pain and what holds you hostage emotionally. Forgive yourself, so you can build your self-esteem and confidence and believe in yourself. Do not carry the weight of guilt, fault and regret from the divorce. Forgive yourself; free yourself of this burden.

I worked with a woman who said she just could not forgive her ex-husband for the hurt and anguish he caused her; by doing so was excusing his bad behavior. After talking with her, I realized she was hung up on the word forgiveness. She was not ready to forgive him and was struggling with letting go. I suggested we find a different word. Once we found one she could associate with, she turned the corner and started taking steps to let go and move forward. This also allowed her to start the process of forgiving herself. If the word forgiveness is not something you are ready to embrace, pick a new word, like absolution, absolve yourself from that person. Or use the word release—release that person from your life.

Let it go. Just let it go... Life will get better, and you can learn to live a new, healthier life. No more "drama trauma," it only holds you hostage. Do not continue to give him control over you and dominate your world. Your relationship needs to move to a new and different level, one you are in control of.

It is time to march forward. Making peace with yourself is liberating and can have a calming effect on you after the storm of divorce. Making peace with yourself will free up energy for you to use in your new journey.

There is a whole world out there. What do you want? What do you want to do? From this point moving forward, it is up to you to decide what and how you are going to live. Being at peace with yourself during this process will help you feel more confident in moving forward and building a new life for yourself. It is time to go boldly into the future.

**Tip:** Forgive yourself and others; do not carry around the negative emotions and waste energy staying angry. Let go of the negative emotions that surround and influence you. Free yourself from negativity and fill the space with positive emotions and feelings.

*Chapter* 16

# SELF-ACCEPTANCE

Self-acceptance is having the confidence to know who you are and letting the world see you for who you are. Do you accept who you are right now? Are you recently divorced and going from being a Mrs. to a Ms., and maybe still figuring out who you are, and where you are headed in life? Your world turned upside down and you are now building a new life for yourself. You can do this—really, what choice do you have? Unless you want to harbor hateful feelings and resentment all of your life, live a "divorce life" or live in a constant state of "drama trauma", accepting who you are is critical. What is more important to you—to be accepted by others or to have self-acceptance? How can others accept you if you do not accept yourself?

Accept yourself, both your faults and good qualities, and pull yourself together. It is time to accept yourself for who you are and not define yourself as someone who is divorced. You are a person first and need to make sure you know who you are and what you want out of life. Accept yourself; know your strengths and use them to move into your new life. You have more strength than you know and are courageous. You are a survivor and cannot be taken down. You took a hit but came back and are still standing. You have faced difficulties and survived. You are important, so think positive things about yourself. Take pride in yourself and what you have accomplished. Accept who you are and where you are in life.

Learn from your mistakes and do not let them hurt or weigh you down moving forward. We are so hard on ourselves. We often talk to ourselves in a negative way. Think about how you would feel if you heard someone say negative, hurtful things about a friend, like you say about yourself. You would be angry or upset. We beat ourselves up, put ourselves down, and are hard on ourselves. We are guilty of cruel treatment toward ourselves. Learn to be respectful of yourself. You are what you tell yourself and become what you hear the most.

When others compliment you, do you say "thank you" or do you discount them and disagree with them? How often have you heard someone compliment someone and the response is negative? For example, if someone says you look nice today and you say, "No I don't," you are actually discounting their feelings. How many times has someone said to you, "That is a beautiful dress; it looks great on you," and you reply, "I hate this dress and it makes me look fat." That response negates their compliment. The next time someone gives you a compliment, say "thank you" and nothing else. It is that simple and you appear more gracious. It turns something nice into something positive about you. This is why self-talk needs to be positive and encouraging to build yourself up, like your friends do for you.

When you look in the mirror, what do you see? Most women look in the mirror and focus on the thing they do not like most about themselves. Do you do that? Go look in the mirror. What is the first thing you notice? Are you having a bad hair day? Have you developed wrinkles around your eyes? Be honest with yourself. Do you see the good things about yourself? How many times do you look in the mirror and think all is good? Have you ever thought this? I encourage you to look in the mirror and say something good, something nice about what you see. Do this for seven days in a row and see if your attitude about yourself begins to change. You must be able to look at yourself and see the good qualities you have and not always focus on the bad. For example, I have good hair. When I look in the mirror and all I see are things I do not like, I make myself focus on my hair. This takes practice, as on bad hair days, I really have to stretch and remember I am blessed with good hair. Find something you like about your appearance, and say something nice to yourself out loud every day while you are looking in the mirror. Look yourself in the eye when you are saying this; it will not be easy. Keep doing it and mean it when you say it. Believe it. This will help build your self-confidence, you will learn to rely on yourself and not others to build you up. Do not put all of your self-confidence and self-esteem in the hands of someone else; it must come from within.

It is hard sometimes to accept or say nice things about yourself. Some see it as being conceited. I am not telling you to go tell others how good you are; I am asking if you know what your good qualities are. Part of self-acceptance is being able to see the good in yourself and not always focus on the bad. Can you list your good qualities right now? Both physically and mentally, list what you like about yourself? Are you kind? Honest? Likeable? Do you have nice legs or good hair? The list can be endless. Below, list your good qualities:

________________________________________________

________________________________________________

________________________________________________

________________________________________________

________________________________________________

________________________________________________

________________________________________________

________________________________________________

How was that? Was it hard? Periodically, check in with yourself and see if you are still accepting of who you are and list good qualities about yourself. Then list things you are working on or want to work on. Being the person you want to be takes work and attention because life is constantly changing, and so should you.

People who are happy lead more productive lives and are healthier. Do you believe you should be happy in life? Or are you jaded by what has happened? Divorce is hard. Accept that you made it through the process or are working through the process. What is your happiness worth? What have you learned about yourself in the process? Trust in yourself and remember at the end of the day, you are still standing. You are tougher and more capable than you give yourself credit for. Part of self-acceptance is being able to laugh at yourself and recognize you will make mistakes. Learn from the mistakes, the mishaps.

Adversity builds character. I often tell people that there are times during adversity when I feel like I am in the cartoon phase of character building. You will have times when you will not like how you react to things or others. This is where learning to respond and not react is helpful. When you react, you are saying or doing whatever first pops into your mind, without thought or filter. During difficult times, reacting can lead to unpleasant encounters, as not so nice things can come right out of your mouth. These may be words or thoughts that you want others to know but maybe not in the manner you pushed them out of your mouth. Learning to respond is better. A response is something you think about and will come out being tactful, even if it is not a pleasant subject.

When faced with something that rattles your control, you might say the first thing that either pops into your head or just comes right out of your mouth without thought. It is always better to think about what you want to say and how you want to say it. If it is not something you would say an hour after the conversation because it is hurtful or mean, then do not say it. If you would not say it the next day, do not say it. This is about you learning to communicate effectively, without remorse.

Learn to control your emotions and not say ugly, hurtful things when you are mad or upset—things you might later regret, not only for what you said, but how you said them. Words spoken in anger usually come back to haunt you. Words spoken in anger hurt people, and if said in the middle of a argument, are usually not really heard anyway as each person is trying to get the other person to hear and understand their point of view. So no one is really listening closely to what is being said, but later remembers the hurtful things. Learn to pause and think before you say anything. You want to respond, not react. This will help you in all aspects of life, as you will learn to control what you say and how you say it. Think about how you want to hear something and respond to others in that fashion. They may not always respond like you want them to, but you will be in control of your emotions and not react. This is about you taking the moral high road and not giving in to fits of rage or having an emotional outburst, which can then be used against you later.

**Tip:** Accept all of yourself, the good and the not-so-good. Accept that you are human and will make mistakes. Talk positively to yourself; build yourself up. Change what you do not like about yourself and learn to love yourself for who you are. Be respectful of yourself and others, even if they are not respectful of you. Be the better person, the person who does not stoop to trash talk just because someone else does. Do not let your ex ignite your anger to the point of becoming ugly and things quickly spiral out of control. Change what you want to change; respond differently than you did before. Accept that you need to change things in your life and within yourself. Learn to accept yourself, faults included, and be the person you want to be.

Chapter 17

# DEFINE YOUR PURPOSE

What is your purpose in life? Why are you here? Do you know what you are supposed to accomplish? Are you on your life's journey? On your self-discovery journey? Are you living up to your potential?

These questions are hard to answer, yet seem to pop up a lot. Do we have to know why we were put on this earth? The answer is: do you want to know? Would knowing the answer help you, in any way, live your life? What if you are on the wrong path?

The answers to these questions all vary depending on where you are at this point in life. If you are still taking steps to move forward and away from the divorce, you may need to continue working through the emotions so you can look toward your future.

Everyone is different with a unique perspective on life; accept where you are in life right now. You may not know the journey ahead, but do you know your passion? It is okay to not know each step along the way, but have a plan. Be realistic as life's details and plans change and you may need to reevaluate your plan. Learn to be flexible and take changes as they come. The end results may stay the same, but the journey to get there can, and will, change. Sometimes life presents a detour such as divorce. You then take a different route to where you are headed to achieve your goals and purpose. You can learn a lot along the way and detours certainly offer times to learn and gain experience and wisdom.

Mistakes are learning opportunities. The more mistakes you make, the more opportunities you have to learn. I tell clients it is better to say it was a learning opportunity or a lesson learned rather than dwelling on making a mistake. What lesson did you learn in the process? You learned something and now it is time to apply what you learned and move on.

Too often, people do not put "wiggle" room in their life plans and get thrown off course when something unexpected happens. Adding wiggle room is knowing the unexpected happens and learning to not let it throw you off your plan. You probably never expected to get a divorce. It is personal, emotional and hard to accept, yet here it is. Now you must accept it, deal with it, and alter your path.

The Merriam-Webster dictionary defines "purpose" as "the reason why something is done or used: the aim or intention of something: the feeling of being determined to do or achieve something: the aim or goal of a person: what a person is trying to do, become, etc."

What is your purpose after the divorce? Do you know the answer to this question? First, you must know what you want and how to achieve it. This is where knowing your strengths can be helpful. What are you really good at? Are you living a life that incorporates using one or more of your strengths? Your life's purpose is what you are here to accomplish. At times it may feel as if you are not living or working toward your purpose. You may have to experience a few lessons learned before you feel like you are on the right path or can even figure out what your purpose is. During a major change in life, you might decide you want to explore different possibilities, and your life journey will take a different path.

It is wonderful to discover new things, see new things and try new things. Life is an adventure; go explore all there is. Discovering new things may help clarify what you really want to accomplish in your life. It can open your eyes to a whole new world and expand your horizons. Life is a journey you travel every day. What have you learned from the journey so far? What lessons have you learned to help move you to the next level? What motivates you to keep moving forward?

Motivation is key to moving forward and exploring what you want to accomplish in your life. This all contributes to your life purpose, to your legacy. At the end of your life, what will you hope to have accomplished? What will you hope people will say about you? You lived a full, happy and productive life? You cared for others? What is your defining contribution to the world? What do you want people to remember about you? This is where your life purpose comes in, to help you live life and enjoy the journey along the way while accomplishing what you are meant to do. You may not always be aware of how you are contributing to your purpose. If you are living life and working toward your goals, while treating people the way you want to be treated, you are working on your life's journey.

Working on yourself, sharing part of yourself and your knowledge with others, and continuing down the road are ways of serving others. Sometimes you will hit a pothole and must detour but, remember, there is a lot to learn on a detour. Notice your surroundings, how you respond not react, as this will help you determine if you are on the right path or need to venture to a new life path. Feeling confident and comfortable in your journey will help you to continue moving forward. Think about your life, see what you want to accomplish, and have the confidence to take steps to make it happen.

**Tip:** Learning is knowledge, and knowledge gives you power and control over your life. When you stop learning, you stop growing.

**Suggestion:** Where are you in your journey? What is your purpose?

SECTION IV:

# CONFIDENCE TO MOVE FORWARD

*Chapter* 18

# CONFIDENCE

Confidence can make you or break you, depending on if you have it or you don't. Confidence can see you through hard times if you believe in yourself and your ability to make it through whatever life throws at you. If you lack confidence, you will stay stuck in one place, and that may be a not-so-nice place to be. During a divorce, you do not want to be stuck forever in the sad, crying phase or the angry stage. If you do not believe in yourself and your confidence has gone on vacation, let's work to get it back.

Confidence will help you make better decisions and know you can and will handle whatever arises. If you are unsure of something, be mature enough to reach out for help. It will help you feel confident to find answers to things you do not know or need help with. It is hard to be confident all of the time, yet it is crucial to your wellbeing. Be confident in knowing when to ask for help and knowing your own limitations. Believing in your abilities and facing the world with confidence is a better plan than facing the world being insecure, and it shows.

Confidence and arrogance are two distinctly different words. Arrogance is believing or acting as if you are superior or more important. Confidence is knowing and believing in yourself and appearing knowledgeable and with self-assurance, certain you can handle things. How people act is a telling sign. How do you act? Are you sure of yourself? Confident that, no matter what happens, you can handle it? Or do you come off as someone who wants to hide out and not be seen?

There are many different ways you can act or appear to others. It is great to appear gracious and confident, even if you are uncertain of the future. You do not have to know what the future holds or the path you will take, but know you can and will handle all you are encountering and move confidently into the future.

Being confident takes courage, class, and clarity and knowing when and how to use these qualities. It takes courage to recognize and acknowledge when you need help, the courage to know you cannot and should not handle things or situations by yourself. It takes courage to admit you do not know something; it takes courage to ask for help when you need it. Asking for help does not make you weak. Having class is knowing whom to ask for help and graciously accepting their help. Being thankful for the help is both classy and respectful, and others will more likely help you in the future if you are thankful.

Clarity means making sure your actions, words and desires are clear to yourself and others. Clarify your thoughts, so you can make your wants and needs known and understood. Be transparent with yourself so you know both what you need help with and how and where to seek that help.

Knowing and appreciating yourself takes courage, class and clarity and will put you on a path to being more confident. You need to believe in yourself to be confident, go from being a worrier to a warrior, and to be your own superhero.

**Tip:** Are you confident? It takes confidence to move forward. What are you most confident about? What does confidence look like to you?

The three C's that make up being Confident:

Courage

Class

Clarity

*Chapter* 19

# Believing in Yourself

Do you believe in yourself? Do you stand firm in your belief? If you do not believe in yourself, why should others?

You teach people how to treat you. If you treat yourself bad, eventually so will others. You set the standard for yourself and show the world who you are. It may be difficult at first to believe in yourself and your abilities following a divorce.

I often hear women say after a divorce their confidence is gone. They couldn't keep or hold their marriage together, so how can they believe in themselves and move confidently into the next phase of their life?

I worked with a client who was sure she was going to end up alone for the rest of her life. She cried all the time yet frequently admitted how terrible her marriage was. She wanted to stay married to a husband who drank too much and was seeing another woman. She attempted several times to try and convince her husband not to leave her. It took its toll on her and she felt worthless.

She handed all of her confidence and self-worth to her husband. Eventually, she glued the pieces of her life together enough to get up every day and face life one day at a time. She had to learn her own self-worth, reclaim her confidence and believe in herself and her ability. The last time I saw her, she looked ten years younger and was happy. She believes in herself again and is confident she can handle whatever life throws at her.

You have to trust in yourself enough to move forward. You have most likely faced adversity before, lived through it by picking yourself up and moving on. It is time to do it again. Yes, this time may be harder, as your personal life has taken a big hit. It is time to work through the emotional divorce baggage, change what you want to change, figure out life lessons and make a plan.

When you are emotional, it is easy to get distracted and veer off the plan you have for yourself. This is why it is important to set goals and have a plan so when you get distracted, you will not stay lost. Pick yourself up and get back on track with your goals. This will move you into a new phase of life—one you navigate, one you put into action.

It is wonderful to believe in yourself and show the world you trust in yourself and your ability. You may not always be right, have the answers, or know what to do, yet it is during these times you build character. How you seek answers or help tells a lot about a person. Believing in yourself takes courage, class, clarity and confidence. Believing in your ability will move you forward in life. Self-reliance is necessary in life, as you need to trust yourself to make decisions and your way through life.

There will be times you may feel others know a better way to handle a situation and you need to trust yourself enough to ask for advice, help, or their thoughts on something. You must believe in your ability, your actions, your reasons for doing something, to believe in yourself. When you doubt yourself, it can quickly turn into questioning yourself and your ability. It is okay to question things in life, but not believing in *you* is not okay. You may question yourself, but do not question believing in yourself.

You only have yourself, so build yourself up, know when to move forward and when to seek help or ask for guidance. This is part of believing in yourself, to have confidence to seek help or the answers, when needed.

When you rely on others for your self-worth, there will always be doubts. You might ask yourself these questions if something is not right: *Did I make them angry? Upset? Are they going to leave?* Then fear sets in, or maybe panic and insecurity. Negative emotions and hurtful feelings can take you to a dark place, one where you doubt yourself. You may even feel unloved or unlovable. You are not unlovable. You are insecure and do not believe in yourself. You are putting other people ahead of yourself, and you do not believe in your own self-worth.

You are worth believing in. At the end of the day, who do you have to rely on? You have yourself. Yes, you have friends and family who you can turn to, but they are not always available. You have to rely on yourself all day, every day and make decisions as to what to do, and act on them. Sometimes this is a scary thought, but you make a lot of decisions every day that affect your life and do not question your actions.

When making life-altering decisions, it comes down to what you want and what is best for you. Do you believe in yourself enough to make the hard decisions? It is great to ask for help and advice, but at the end of the day, it is your life; therefore, you decide what you need to do. Seek guidance and find the knowledge or information you need. It is better to make an informed decision than to make a split- second decision affecting the rest of your life. This is your life, and you need to decide what you want to do. If you do not believe in yourself and have someone else make the decisions for you, you only have yourself to blame if it does not work out. It is easier to blame someone else than to take responsibility; however, you have to live with the consequences.

A perfect example of this is if you listen to your friends, who are not family law attorneys, tell you what you need to do in your case, instead of listening to your attorney. Friends mean well but, remember, there are laws and rules that have to be followed, and it may not always seem right or fair. If you end up dragging out the divorce and/or spending more money on the divorce because you decided to fight for something you felt wasn't fair, you are the one who has to face the consequences. Even if the law is very clear on this matter, because you did not trust yourself enough and listened to your friend, you have no one but yourself to blame.

Oftentimes your instincts are on point, but during times of emotional duress it is easy to second-guess yourself if someone disagrees with you. Seek advice and listen to those you trust, but ultimately the decision is yours. Believing in yourself, whether you make good or bad decisions, is about you taking control over your life and living life your way. Again, making informed decisions is best. This is your life and you have to live with the decisions you make and things you do. You know yourself better than anyone, so believe in yourself and make the best decisions you can. Take responsibility for yourself and your actions.

Do you love yourself? You accept love from others by how you love yourself or show others how to love you. We lead by example; other people see what we do and follow accordingly. I am going to ask again; do you love yourself? Or has fear and insecurity taken a toll on you? You must examine how you see and present yourself to others. If you are always putting yourself down, other people see and hear it. Disrespecting yourself shows others you do not believe in yourself.

This is not how you want the world to see you. It is time to discover things about yourself, find out who you are, where you are going, what you want or need, and to change. It is not always an easy path; however, you will learn a lot about yourself on this journey. Do not be fearful of learning who you are, as you can change whatever you do not like and enhance the things you do like.

Believe in yourself and your dreams. You must have courage and confidence to believe in yourself and make changes in your life. To actually live in a fulfilling manner, you must accept who you are and show the world who you are. Trust in yourself. You may not always like what happens, but when you believe and trust in yourself enough to know you can handle anything, amazing things can happen.

**Tip:** Take steps to realize and accept good decisions and things you have done. Remember you can and will handle things, so believe in yourself. Make a conscious effort to acknowledge your strengths. I encourage you to make a list of things you have accomplished to remind yourself that you can handle things. Always, *always* believe in yourself.

List a situation that was difficult yet you handled:

## Chapter 20

# From Worrier to Warrior

How many times has worrying stopped you from doing something? Worrying can take over your life, and what does it cost you?

Well, everything really. Worrying, just like fear, can hold you hostage and cause you to doubt yourself and have a mindset of limiting beliefs. Worrying can exhaust your mental energy and drain you, leaving you weak and still worried about what you were originally worried about. Worrying can make you lose focus. Does that worry you? If not, it should. Most of the time when you worry about something, how does it turn out? More often than not, things work out fine. Then what do you have to show for yourself? Drained energy and lost time.

During a divorce, you probably felt like you were in a battle most of the time, and your mindset determined how you got through the difficult times. Did you cry and worry, or were you a Warrior? Instead of worrying so much, become a Warrior. A Warrior fights for what they believe in, stands guard, and handles things as they happen. They are always prepared to handle situations, even the unexpected. A Warrior believes in their abilities, knows life can and will knock you down, but a Warrior gets back up. A Warrior is strong, protective, and known for having courage and skill. A Warrior depends on themselves and other Warriors for their skill, experience and confidence.

When engaged in conflict, you do not need to be a worrier, you need to be a Warrior! Stand up for yourself! Be tough! Depend on yourself, your skill, experience and confidence. We have all been engaged in some form of battle, and a divorce is an emotional battle.

Do not face the world worrying about every little detail, as you will get lost in the little things and not see the big picture. You need to depend on yourself, the Warrior. Have the confidence and courage to face the opposition and not stand down, not be afraid or let fear hold you back. Believe in yourself and your ability to handle things. A Warrior is brave and stands up for herself. This is about being you and doing what you want and not worrying what other people think.

Do not fight for the sake of fighting, but be strategic and smart and fight for what you really want. Let go of things unimportant to you. Never start a battle unless it is absolutely necessary; try to resolve things amicably first. Battle is the last option. Warriors know when and how to hold and keep control. They do not let emotions rule their world and do not give in to worry. Worrying does not accomplish anything, except drain your energy and time. Isn't it better to drain your energy by accomplishing something instead of sitting back and worrying? You must trust and believe in yourself enough to take care of yourself, to be a Warrior.

Remember, you have been through tough times before, and you are still standing. The same can be said about the divorce; you will still be standing at the end. Yes, you might have battle wounds. Yes, you might think your life will never be the same, and that is correct. You will not be the same, as your life has changed. It does not mean you need to stop living. It simply means your life has changed. Take steps to make this change a time to reflect, regroup and move forward in a new, positive way. You may get knocked down, but get up, dust yourself off and keep moving. Do not let worry or anyone else control or dictate your life. You are a Warrior. Take control of your life.

**Tip:** You will stumble, so prepare yourself to stand strong and handle whatever comes your way. You may not always know what to do, but believe you can and will handle it. You have seen battles before and survived, and you will survive this one. Believe in yourself and your ability—be a mighty Warrior!

*Chapter* 21

# Be Your Own Superhero

If you had a super power, what would it be? What superhero would you emulate? Do you want to be Superman and fly? Be Spiderman and have super strength and agility? Or maybe be like Wonder Woman, and save and rescue not only yourself but others? Did you know Wonder Woman is a warrior princess of the Amazons of Greek mythology? Wonder Woman has strength, ability and quick actions. Do you see yourself in any of these descriptions?

I hope you do. If not, it is time to get busy and realize your strengths and power. What actions have you taken in the past that you or others needed? This can help you determine your own strengths. You have the power to make things happen in your life. There are times you may not feel that you have the power to continue the struggle or fight the battle before you. Do you really have an option? The only other option is to give in, lie down, and let life steamroll you. Is that what you want? Probably not. Even in the worst of times, when emotions are running high, find and use your abilities and powers, and do not give your power to others.

Being your own superhero means you can and will handle and tackle anything life throws at you. You can take on the ugly, messy side of life and stay attentive to your own needs. Rescue yourself from a life of worry and unhappiness, a life of pain, regret or anger. Rescue yourself if you are not being loved or if you are not being fulfilled.

Empower yourself, and do not depend on others to always take care of you. When you give away your power, you are dependent upon others and are not in control of your life. Yes, there are times we all need help, but how often do you rely on others instead of relying on yourself? You are smart, bright, resourceful, and knowledgeable. You can handle life, so take charge of your life. Be your own superhero, take care of yourself, and show the world who you are.

You need to take care of yourself so you can care for and help others. Part of being your own superhero is taking care of yourself as you would care for others. Remember to not only fight for liberty and justice for others, but also for yourself. The key is to take care of yourself and to not depend on others to always take care of all of your needs. Yes, let others help you in time of need, but do not sit curled up in a ball, or hide under the covers, afraid. Know who you are, what your strengths are and how to use them. Know when you need time to re-charge and rest so you can be the best version of yourself. Let your strengths and knowledge guide you so you can tackle problems as they arise. Take time for yourself when times are tough, then gather your strength and take care of what needs to be done. Do not give your power to others because, if you do, you will always be a damsel in distress. And who wants to be that person?

Be aware, believe in yourself and manage your own life. Empower yourself to live your life and make decisions for yourself. Empower yourself to take care of yourself.

What are your strengths? What are you really good at? All of these characteristics contribute to your superpowers. Be aware, and use these powers to tackle life's problems. You do not want to end up kidnapped by The Joker, waiting on Batman, Superman, or some other superhero to come rescue you. You are bright, intelligent, and resourceful. You can figure out how to find and keep your freedom, find yourself and your strength. Having the confidence to know you are your own superhero is liberating!

**Tip:** What kind of superhero are you? What are your superpowers? Give yourself a superhero name. I know it sounds strange, but it can give you the confidence you need to call yourself by your superhero name when you need to give yourself a boost.

My superhero name is: ________________________________

SECTION V:

# LIVE *YOUR* LIFE

## *Chapter* 22

# LIVING LIFE

Living life is both difficult and wonderful all rolled into one. If I asked if you are living life, or are you living *YOUR* life, what would the answer be? Are you aware of living your own life? Or are you simply surviving, living day to day? Do you have dreams? Are you living your dreams? What are you dreams? Have you written them down, defined them?

Do you have a plan? Are you working on a plan to *live YOUR* life? Are you taking steps to live your dream? Or are you just existing, trying to please everyone else?

It is time to take inventory of yourself and how you are living. It is time to ask yourself hard and sometimes painful questions, so you know where you stand right now and where you want to be. What obstacles or roadblocks are in the way of you reaching your goals? What hurdles have you put in your own way? It is time to assume your superhero persona, face reality, make a plan and put steps in place to forge ahead. There is no time like the present to review, revise, modify and revamp your life.

Are you living in the present, or are you still living through the "what if's..." and "if only..." phase? It is important to work through the emotions and be able to make progress in life. As you work through the emotions, be aware of taking steps forward and celebrate your success along the way. It is important to acknowledge the emotions you have worked through and be aware of the changes happening in your life. Celebrate the good times, and learn from the hard times. If you stop learning, you stop growing. Self-acknowledgement is not grandiose; it is an important step in knowing who you are, what you are capable of, accepting who you are, and loving yourself. It will give you the confidence to live life the way you want to live.

Part of living *YOUR* life is knowing when to ask for help and to seek guidance and help when you need it. Learn from others. Take what you learn and apply it to your life. Change it or modify it to work in your life. Your life is not the exact same as someone else's life. Know you are not alone and are capable of taking care of yourself and living your life.

We are all unique. We have wants and needs that are different, or look different, than what others may want for us. Friends and family all want the best for you, but what they envision for you may not be what you envision for yourself. You need to be able to clearly state what you want in life and work toward obtaining and living that life. It may take years to get to the point that you are actually living your life the way you want it to be. If it does take a while, keep your eyes focused on you and what you want to achieve. Do not lose focus. You will learn new things along the way. Be flexible as your needs and wants may change, and adjust your expectations along the way. Life is a journey you live every day, so make the most of it. You cannot get back lost time, so be present, live in the moment, and enjoy the journey.

This is your life, so be courageous and stand up for yourself. Do not let others derail you. During and after a divorce, it is important to not let your ex-spouse or the situation drag you down. It was rough and life was difficult, now it is *YOUR* time. Time to live *YOUR* life. Do not let others drain your energy or hold you back. Do not let unpleasant or unexpected situations hold you hostage. Push through the hard and difficult times. Take a time out if needed to recharge, work through what you need to and get back up and live. Life is what you make it to be, so take charge of your life. Do not hold yourself back. Learn the importance of having fun, be spontaneous, adventuresome and discover new things. Enjoy life.

Life may knock you down at times and when it does, get right back up. You have been knocked down before and lived through it. You will get back up this time. Take time to work through situations and emotions so they will not hold you back. Dream about what you want and who you want to be. Focus on you and make your dreams a reality. This dream is about you succeeding in life, not getting revenge on your ex-spouse. If you want revenge, you are channeling negative emotions and energy and your focus is not on you. Wanting or trying to prove to others you can move on will get you started on the moving-on cycle. Yet it needs to be about you and for you, not to prove to others you are capable of moving forward. In the beginning, it may have been the energy to move you to take stock of your life. At some point, your reason for change needs to be to prove to yourself you can. This is about you and your life. Believe in yourself and your ability and grow confident in yourself. This is your life. Try new things, go bravely into your new life. It can be an adventure if you have the right attitude.

Visualize yourself being confident. What does it look like? What does it feel like? What does living a life you imagined and dream about look like? How can you change your life to live your dreams? What do you need to do to live your life and not merely survive? Channel these feelings when needed and use your strength, energy, superpowers and survival instincts to motivate, activate and participate in your life.

**Tip:** Enjoy yourself and live. Live life, and smile every morning as the day holds many adventures. Every day is a new day. Do not let troubles prevent you from enjoying life. Be thankful and grateful for life. Live your life, the one you dream about and have worked for.

*Chapter* 23

# MOTIVATE

What motivates you? What kicks you in gear to do something? Hopefully you will NOT say, "So I can show HIM that I am not __ (lazy, unlovable, or whatever word you feel works, as revenge is not an admirable strategy). Hopefully, what spurs you on is the desire to know who you are and what you want and to take the steps necessary to achieve your dream and live *YOUR* life. A life you have control over, a plan that suits you and what you want to achieve.

What motivates you? A sense of duty, a purpose, or an end result? What will motivate you to make changes, maybe even drastic changes? What is the incentive to change? Is it not living your life tied to the past and hoping for a different outcome? Review your purpose and take steps to achieve your purpose. Imagine yourself, one step at a time, moving up the staircase, leading you to your new life, a life you have a plan for and exists because of you.

Let's look at this from a different perspective. Life is like a grand staircase that you are gracefully ascending. If you skip a step, you miss important lessons and actions. Skip two or three steps and you seem to be moving quickly up the staircase; however, moving too quickly can cause you to trip, fall, and tumble to the bottom. Maybe you stumbled but continue to move toward the top, only to be sidetracked by the bannister. Imagine how fun it would be to hop on and slide down, how thrilling, see– I can have fun! You then find yourself at the bottom of the staircase again, looking up. If you find yourself starting the journey again, what would entice you to start up the staircase again?

You could stumble and fall or get sidetracked again. (The slide down the bannister was fun…) Maybe you sit on the bottom step and contemplate what you really want. Do you want to always live at the bottom of the stairs, or get halfway up the staircase, reach a landing and stop? Do you start the journey up the stairs, taking your time with each step, to make sure you are secure before taking the next step?

Do you know what your own personal speed is: slow and steady, or moving at a faster pace? Travel at whatever speed works for you. When you move at your own personal speed, each step of the journey will provide life lessons to propel you to the next step. The motivation should be to learn along the way and continue to strive to move to the next step. Each step brings you closer to reaching the top, your goal and life purpose.

Now is the time to discover what motivates you and create a realistic plan to begin the journey of reaching your destination- living *YOUR* life. Check in with yourself periodically, reevaluate where you are and where you want to go. Life throws detours, enjoy the scenery along the way. If you get sidetracked, change the plan to include setbacks or sidetracks. Do not be so rigid that it throws you off track. Learn to be flexible, or as I like to say, add in wiggle room, as long as it doesn't hurt or completely distract you. Check in with yourself and celebrate the little things, as this can help motivate you to continue your journey. Plan time to stop and think, to examine how much you are changing. Give yourself time to enjoy the journey. It is more fun that way.

**Tip:** What motivates you? If you do not know, find out and rely on it to keep you going. Write a goal on a sticky note and post it where you can see it every day. Once you achieve that goal, write out the next goal and continue doing so. This keeps you focused on one goal, one step at a time.

What motivates you to achieve your goals?

Chapter 24

# ACTIVATE

You should have your plan outlined and all ready to move forward, as it is now time to activate the plan. Are you prepared? Are you ready to set your plan into action? Did you plan and gather the supplies needed to move forward? Are you mentally, emotionally and physically ready to activate your plan? It is time to start your journey and take the first step toward personal independence. Put on your superhero persona, place one foot forward, and begin the journey. Now is the time to spark and crank up your energy. With your plan in place and with self-motivation, you are ready to begin.

What does this step look like to you? In your plan, did you visualize the journey? The destination? Start moving and remember to take time with each step because you want to live in each moment. You want to participate in each step, to touch, feel and learn from the journey. Activate your plan and your senses as you will want to *experience* life, *YOUR* life. Anytime you feel stuck or as if you cannot go on, reach out to your emotional support team. Let them help you work through what triggered the stall and get you moving again. Know you are not alone on this journey. Your emotional support team is your cheering section, and they will help propel you forward if you are stuck or need a boost. Let your team, your cheerleaders, energize you when needed and gently push you to take the next step.

You are smart, have set goals for yourself and, at times, may feel as if you have slid down the bannister. If so, round up your cheerleaders and put yourself back in action. This does not have to be done at a speed not easy for you. We all have our own personal speed limit, the speed at which we feel comfortable accomplishing things. If you are stuck in the slow lane and need to pick it up a notch, ask your emotional support team to push you a little and to hold you accountable. Sometimes all you need is a boost. If you are stuck in the fast lane and things are moving so quickly that life is a blur, change lanes. Slow it down, if only temporarily. Remember to enjoy the scenery along the way. Figure in detours, traffic, and life's potholes. Things happen and you may be slowed down by other people's actions or by life. If so, take it in stride, but do not quit. Continue on your journey. Stay the course.

**Tip:** Time to activate your new life plan and move forward, one step at a time. Ready, set, ACTION!

List one ACTION you are ready to address right now:

______________________________________________

______________________________________________

______________________________________________

______________________________________________

# Chapter 25

# PARTICIPATE

Are you ready to participate in *YOUR* life? I sure hope so! You have a plan, are motivated, and have activated the plan. Next, it is time to participate, to share your life with others, and to enjoy being *you*. Acceptance of yourself is essential and will help motivate you to participate in your own life. You need to create a life that is exciting, challenging and comforting to you. You want to be excited to wake up and face each new day. Even during tough times, if you are participating in life, it is easier to face whatever life throws at you. Having a positive mindset makes life easier to deal with.

Participating in life means to live, to be active, to function, to focus and enjoy life. Now is the time to get out more, to socialize. Go out with friends for dinner, to a gallery opening, a museum or see a movie or play. You need to get out of the house and start functioning in a social setting. Now is a great time to do something that you have always wanted to do but have not done. Go sign up for a dance, pottery, or cooking class. Take a wine tasting class. Go back to school. Take up yoga or knitting. Or try something completely different—skydiving? Volunteer at a homeless shelter, animal shelter, your favorite charity, or a hospital. Stretch the boundaries of your comfort zone. You may learn you have held yourself back from doing something you thought was scary only to discover you really enjoy doing it. Time to be adventuresome and experience life, even if it is taking it one step at a time. You have been through an ordeal and so much has changed. Take this part slow, get comfortable with each new step. Build up your self-esteem and believe in yourself.

This is also a good time, if you are ready, to think about dating. Which means you have to put yourself out there. Are you ready to put yourself out there? Ready to go out and meet other people? Are you ready to pay attention to others, in a dating sense? If the idea does not frighten or make you uncomfortable, it is time to explore the dating world.

Start out slow and easy, maybe meet someone for coffee or lunch. Go out with friends in a group to ease back into the social dating arena. Find someone who has similar interests to do things with, and see where it takes you. Now is the time to open up new avenues for yourself. If you are not ready to date, find a friend or companion to go do things with. You need to figure out who you are and what you want before you start dating. Make a list of the qualities you are attracted to and a list of what you want in a relationship. These two lists may surprise you at how different they are. Take time to determine what you want in a new relationship. New you, new expectations. If you are attracted to the same type of person you just divorced, you have not worked through the emotions and changed. If you are not careful, you will get involved with the same type of person as your ex, just with a different name. I often call this attraction "repeat offenders" as you are drawn to someone because they are familiar in their mannerism, personality or physical appearance. You divorce Billy and marry Bob. Same man, different name.

I have seen women marry the same type of man the second time around trying to fix what was wrong in the first marriage, and it does not end well. You cannot fix the past. You can only change the present and move forward. If the sole reason you date someone is because they are the complete opposite of your ex-spouse, it will not end well. This line of reasoning proves you have not worked out the emotional baggage from your divorce. You are just moving in a different direction thinking or hoping it will work. This decision can lead to a whole new set of issues if you have not worked out what happened in the first marriage and are just expecting the next man to be perfect. Everyone comes with baggage; it is how the person *manages* the baggage that is important.

You must put in time to figure out who you are, what you want, and how to get there. This is also true in looking for a new partner or relationship. You need to be aware of your wants, needs and desires before starting a new relationship. If you are still reeling from the divorce, you need to process the changes that have been made and that still need to be made before starting to date. It is not a good idea to date and be influenced by someone else, a possible partner, when you are still fragile from the emotional roller coaster of divorce.

When you do begin to date, I caution you to not compare everyone to your ex-spouse. If you do, you are not ready to date and are still carrying around your emotional divorce baggage. Proceed with caution, keep your eyes open and do not settle because you are scared of being alone. You need to be comfortable with yourself and being alone before you start dating.

Ideally, you want to be in a relationship because you want to, not because you need to. Any new relationship should complement you, not hold you back. If you have to change yourself, or cannot be yourself with this new person, move on. Do not change for someone else, only change for yourself. If someone asks you to change something to suit their needs, run as fast as you can away from this person!

Dating after a divorce is tricky, scary and exciting at the same time. After being married, it is tough to "date" as you have been close and intimate and now may feel like an awkward teenager. The dating rules have changed. It is time to try new things and, if you do not like something, you do not have to do it.

This is *YOUR* life and you get to decide what you want to do. Be open to new things, try new restaurants, discover places in the area you live in and did not know about. Go to events in your city, meet new people, expand your horizons. This can be an exciting time to learn new things about yourself, what you like and what you do not like. Now is your time to focus on you and what you want to do.

Participate in life. The time is going to pass anyway so you might as well enjoy the journey. Do not let stress and troubles weigh you down, which is hard to do at times. Fear and stress can hold you back and keep you stuck. This is not living; it is merely surviving. It is time to open up to experience life and all it has to offer. This is *YOUR* life; it is up to you to live it. Do you want to look back on your life and regret time you wasted being fearful? Or look back and realize you let the divorce run or even ruin your life?

No, you need to take steps to deal with the emotions to fully participate in your life's journey, to enjoy each step along the way. Take life as it happens and participate in it. Do not shut down. This is *YOUR* life, and you need to be the star of it. You are the best at being you, so expand your horizons and participate in life. It is up to you to do the things you want to do.

Plan things to do, get moving, be social, and have fun. Life is too short to stay stuck in hurt and anger. This is *YOUR* life… what do you want to do with it?

**Tip:** You must participate to enjoy living life. Learn new things, experience all life has to offer!

List activities you are ready to try:

________________________________________

________________________________________

________________________________________

________________________________________

________________________________________

________________________________________

________________________________________

________________________________________

________________________________________

________________________________________

# CLOSING THOUGHTS

You get to choose if you are going to live *YOUR* life or merely survive. Life is a lot more satisfying when you enjoy it. You need to work through your emotions and feelings to be able to fully live and enjoy life. Life is too short to be unhappy. You face challenges and choices every day and need to decide how to handle them. You can take action or do nothing and face the consequences later. It is your choice, your decision. Now is the time to focus on you, do what you want to do, live *YOUR* life.

Life has taken you on an emotional roller coaster ride and it is time to get off. It is time for you to find out who you are, what you want, what stops you, what triggers certain emotions. Make a plan to move forward and take life one step at a time. Work through the emotions and feelings, change your attitude, and be grateful for the good things in your life. Being confident is a great feeling and can help navigate you through life. Make peace with yourself and let go of the negative feelings; accept who you are. Define your purpose, discover your strengths, become a Warrior and your own super-hero. This is your life, and you need to be in control of it.

You must motivate, activate and participate in life. You must believe and trust in yourself. Remember you will have good days and bad days. After working through the emotional divorce baggage, bad days will turn into bad moments, and then simply just bad memories.

Take this time to learn things about yourself and get to know who you really are. It is not selfish to take time for yourself. It is necessary and vital to your health and life. You will discover things about yourself. You have good qualities and your own personal superpowers! You are a wonderful person who has a lot to offer, so spend time getting to know who you are at this point in your life. Love yourself and enjoy spending time with yourself.

Find out what you want in life, and what you want in a relationship before you begin a new one. It is important to know what you want in a partner before you find one. It is time to find out what is important to you. Do not settle for less than you deserve, or simply put—do not settle. Time to explore new opportunities for yourself, try new things and discover things you did not know about yourself. Time to go boldly into the future.

Do not let the past hold you down, and do not live chained to your past. Learn from mistakes and move forward. What happened in your past will not repeat itself if you change your life and your expectations. Be realistic yet stretch yourself. Move beyond your comfort zone and explore all that life has to offer.

Do not let the divorce define you. Just because you are divorced, it does not mean your life is over. It is time to move into the next phase in your life. Yes, there will be hard times, sad times, anger and hurt to contend with. There is not a quick, easy cure or fix. You must address and work through the emotional divorce baggage, or it will control you and fear will hold you hostage. Confront and work through your feelings, journal and/or seek professional help to get it all out. Then have a journal burning bonfire and let the anger and hurt go up in flames, never to return.

Work through the emotions. Do not live in negative emotions and ruin the next phase of your life. Acceptance is not always easy, as this is not how you believed your life would turn out. The reality is, you are getting a divorce, or are divorced. You can accept this or live in the past; it is your choice. Let go of the negative people in your life and those who do not support you in your new journey. Appreciate and be thankful for your emotional support team, who have walked with you on this journey and only want the best for you. You have a lot of life ahead of you and so much to live for. Choose yourself and start a new life journey.

It takes time and courage to face the emotions, but it is worth it so you can live a happy, joyful life. Live a life of gratitude and be thankful for the many blessings in your life. Start each day with a smile. It is a new day and new adventures await you. Be positive, courageous and adventuresome; expand your horizons.

Follow your dreams, desires, and ambitions. There is so much life ahead of you. Go live *YOUR* life. There is a whole world out there. What do *you* want?

Finally: Choose Happy! Happiness is a choice.

# REFERENCES AND RESOURCES

Below is a list of books, articles, and assessments you can find online to help you with your journey of self-discovery:

Strengths Finder 2.0 Assessment. Find out your top 5 strengths and how to effectively use them. http://www.strengthsfinder.com/

*Stand Out* by Marcus Buckingham. This book can help you build awareness and potential.

Emotional Intelligence. Knowing your EQ will help you recognize your own as well as other people's emotions. http://www.talentsmart.com/test/

Authentic Happiness Test. Learn about positive psychology and measure your overall happiness. http://www.authentic-happiness.com/home/Discover-Your-Strengths

*How to Fascinate* by Sally Hogshead. Find out your natural fascination strength. This test measures how the world sees you. http://howtheworldseesyou.com/fascination-advantage-assessment/

Each of these resources can uncover insights about you. You will learn things about yourself or be reminded of your strengths and passions. It is good to know and can help you in discovering who you want to be.

**Footnotes:**

[1] Excerpt from the song *New Attitude* sung by Patti LaBelle, from the album Live! One Night Only, released December 1984. Song written by Sharon Teresa Robinson, Jon Gilutin and Bunny Hill.

# TIPS AND SUGGESTIONS

- First, make a list of the behaviors you want to change; be specific. Next, create a detailed, step-by-step plan on the actions you are going to take to change those behaviors.

- What are you good at? What are your strengths? Know the importance of being aware of who you are, what you can do (accomplish) and do not let obstacles (fear) stop you. Life is changing, so advance with change; do not just roll with it. You are now responsible for yourself and your household. What changes do you need to make to take care of things? Make a list of at least three of your strengths and three changes you want to make in your life.

- Manage your emotions, or they will run your life and not in a good, productive way. Seek guidance to help you deal with the emotional upheaval. You do not have to weather this transition alone.

- How do you keep from letting the divorce take over and run your life? Here are some tips that can be helpful:
  1. Seek the help of a professional, someone who specializes in divorce, who can help you manage the emotions running through your mind and running your life. Someone to hold you accountable, help you handle the issues and not stay stuck in the emotions and problems.

2. Have a select group of people, your inner circle, your emotional support group, and let them help you. People who will listen, offer advice and tell you the hard truths. Remember you do not have to follow their advice, but if you lean on them, they want to help and will offer words of wisdom and tell you what they think you should do. You need to have someone to "vent" to, so you can release the emotions.
3. Get into a new routine as soon as possible. You are now responsible for taking care of everything in your house whereas before maybe each spouse took care of certain tasks. Now is the time to establish new habits and a new daily routine. We are all creatures of habit although we do not like to admit it. The faster you get back into a routine, the less time you will have to worry about why things are not getting done and then feel overwhelmed.
4. Be aware of your emotions and feelings and how you react to others around you. Be mindful of how you treat yourself.
5. If you are still in the divorce process, work with your attorney to move the case along; do not let the case stall due to lack of work on your part. The sooner you are through with the process, the quicker you can start your new life.
6. Start working on something you want to change about yourself, whether it is starting a new exercise program or taking a class. You need to stay busy and not let your mind linger on the divorce. If you have too much time on your hands and nothing to do, then you might spend the time dwelling on the divorce and all the baggage it brings. This is not a healthy place to be.

- Move your body, exercise, eat nutritionally, redecorate, be adventuresome and try new things.

- Learn to manage your emotions, or they will manage you. Seek help to work through your emotions. Buy a journal or notebook to write down your thoughts and feelings.

- Be realistic in your expectations. Manage your expectations, or reality will manage them for you.

- Do what you can to minimize the lonely times. Spend time with friends and family to fill up the lonely times. Do not let yourself sink down into depression.

- Life is better and easier to handle when you have a positive attitude. Remember: change your attitude, change your life.

- Look at the big picture; it will help you make better decisions. Focus on what is really important, and do not get caught up in the little details that really do not mean much to you.

- Being grateful is good for your health and well-being. Living in gratitude can help you to not take things for granted, and it can change your perspective. With this in mind, make a daily list of at least three things for which you are grateful. During difficult times, you may need to list a few more things to change your attitude to one of gratefulness. And remember: there is always something to be grateful for.

- Journaling is a good way to get emotions out, discover what is bothering you and work through it. Get the emotions out of your head and onto paper. It can release feelings of being overwhelmed, and it is a good way to let out and let go of your negative emotions. Be grateful for the little things in life—they add up once you become aware of them.

- Faith, prayer, truth and hope will see you through every minute of your life. Remember, you are never alone in this journey.

- Forgive yourself and others; do not carry around the negative emotions and waste energy staying angry. Let go of the negative emotions that surround and influence you. Free yourself from negativity and fill the space with positive emotions and feelings.

- Accept all of yourself, the good and the not-so-good. Accept that you are human and will make mistakes. Talk positively to yourself; build yourself up. Change what you do not like about yourself and learn to love yourself for who you are. Be respectful of yourself and others, even if they are not respectful of you. Be the better person, the person who does not stoop to trash talk just because someone else does. Do not let your ex ignite your anger to the point of becoming ugly and things quickly spiral out of control. Change what you want to change; respond differently than you did before. Accept that you need to change things in your life and within yourself. Learn to accept yourself, faults included, and be the person you want to be.

- Learning is knowledge, and knowledge gives you power and control over your life. When you stop learning, you stop growing.

- Are you confident? It takes confidence to move forward. What are you most confident about? What does confidence look like to you?

  The three C's that make up being Confident:

  Courage

  Class

  Clarity

- Take steps to realize and accept good decisions and things you have done. Remember you can and will handle things, so believe in yourself. Make a conscious effort to acknowledge your strengths. I encourage you to make a list of things you have accomplished to remind yourself that you can handle things. Always, *always* believe in yourself.

- You will stumble, so prepare yourself to stand strong and handle whatever comes your way. You may not always know what to do, but believe you can and will handle it. You have seen battles before and survived, and you will survive this one. Believe in yourself and your ability—be a mighty Warrior!

- What kind of superhero are you? What are your superpowers? Give yourself a superhero name. I know it sounds strange, but it can give you the confidence you need to call yourself by your superhero name when you need to give yourself a boost.

- Enjoy yourself and live. Live life, and smile every morning as the day holds many adventures. Every day is a new day. Do not let troubles prevent you from enjoying life. Be thankful and grateful for life. Live your life, the one you dream about and have worked for.

- What motivates you? If you do not know, find out and rely on it to keep you going. Write a goal on a sticky and post it where you can see it every day. Once you achieve that goal, write out the next goal, and continue doing so. This keeps you focused on one goal, one step at a time.

- Time to activate your new life plan and move forward, one step at a time. Ready, set, ACTION!

- You must participate to enjoy living life. Learn new things, experience all life has to offer!

- Sing along to the song, *New Attitude* by Patti LaBelle, or sing along to whatever song puts you in a good mood, one that can change your attitude for the better.

# SOME THINGS TO CONSIDER

Divorce is hard and takes its toll on everyone, so to lighten things up and hopefully make you laugh, here are a few funny, yet true, thoughts for you to consider:

1. No one is keeping you awake because they are snoring (unless your dog snores and sleeps in your room).
2. No one is breathing heavily or talking in their sleep (unless your dog is a deep breather…)
3. No one is tooting and smelling up the room, or childishly holding your head under the covers when they do.
4. No one is stealing all of the covers.
5. You can keep the temperature of the house how you like it—no more freezing you out, or sweating. You control the thermostat now.
6. TV on or off? Your choice, and you have control of the remote so you can watch whatever you want.
7. You can and should get all new bedding in the colors you want, no more compromising. Maybe a wonder woman theme…
8. You can sleep in the middle of the bed with as many pillows as you want.
9. You can sleep in a granny nightgown or an old comfy shirt.
10. You can stay up as late as you want with the light on, or go to sleep as early as you want.

11. You can wake up and watch TV or read, without having to worry about morning breath or what your hair looks like.
12. You can hang out in your pajamas all day and not worry about what you look like.
13. You can eat anytime you want and eat anything you want, no more waiting to eat together. (A scoop of peanut butter straight off the spoon is always a good dinner choice…)
14. You can have the whole closet to yourself.
15. You can buy as many pairs of shoes as you want and do not have to worry about what will be said about it.
16. You can take up the whole bathroom counter if you want.
17. Your grocery bill will go down (especially if you eat peanut butter for dinner).
18. The man cave can now be used as your craft room.
19. No more running out of hot water in the shower.
20. Not as much laundry to do.

This list is done in jest, and I hope you laughed while reading it. It offers a new perspective on some issues to put a smile on your face.

# MELISSA'S DIVORCE TERMINOLOGY

**Divorce diet**: not hungry, eat very little, and/or so stressed that weight just falls off.

**Drama trauma**: creating drama out of everything happening and making it very traumatic in the process.

**Emotional divorce baggage**: all of the emotions and feelings you experience from the breakup of your marriage and carry with you throughout the divorce.

**Emotional price tag**: the price you pay, both mentally and physically, to deal with high emotions and feelings.

**Fear**: Forward Energy at Rest

**From Mrs. to Ms.**: when you get divorced and become a single person again and are no longer part of a couple. You are now responsible for yourself and your own actions.

**Guilt-bully cycle of life**: when you feel guilt and then bully those around you to make up for your negative or bad feelings, or to either guilt or bully someone to get your way.

**Guilt wagon**: when you feel so guilty you are paralyzed. You feel so bad that you do things for others that you should not, just to try to appease others and cover up what you are feeling.

**Hard truth:** hearing something that is difficult to hear or comprehend, yet is true.

**If only**: when you are struggling to let go someone or something and often state a phrase you wish could change the outcome and take things back to another time.

**Lessons learned**: learning something through experience.

**Life lessons**: something learned the hard way or through making a mistake.

**Living a "divorce life"**: letting the divorce consume all and every aspect of your life. You cannot focus on anything else and will tell anyone and everyone who listens all the sordid details. You cannot or will not move on from the divorce.

**Move forward**: to live your life and make progress in life. To not be stuck in one place or situation.

**Not today day:** a day when you have had enough of the world and need to stay in, not do much and give yourself a break so you can change your attitude and outlook. A day to refresh yourself so you have a better, more positive outlook.

**Own personal speed limit**: the speed at which you are comfortable moving and doing things in life. Every one moves at their own speed.

**Poor me**: when you blame someone else for everything, tell everyone how wronged you were, feel as if no one loves you and you feel sorry for yourself.

**Repeat offender**: when you are attracted to the same type of person you were married to. You are drawn to someone because they are familiar in mannerism, personality or physical appearance. Same person, different name.

**What if's**: when you are stuck living in the past and cannot let go and often begin sentences or statements with this phrase to imagine how things could have been.

**Wiggle room**: when you add in time or space for something to change and it does not throw your day, mood or attitude off. We all need to incorporate more of this into our daily life.

# ACKNOWLEDGMENTS

There are so many people to thank and so many memories and emotions, many of which are not all so pretty, but together they made me into the person I am today. I have stumbled and fallen and picked myself up with the help of many loving friends and family. This book is a testament to my faith and the love and support of many. I want to express my gratitude for the people in my life who have supported me, encouraged me, and pushed me to become me.

To my wonderful, loving husband, Gary, who has supported me through many trials and tribulations. We have laughed, cried, and experienced many adventures together; he is my rock. He has encouraged me to write this book for years, and I am forever grateful for his support, but mostly for his love. Thank you, Honey; I love you more.

Jay, you are a wonderful son, and I am blessed to be your Mom. May we always dance in the kitchen. Thank you for your love, support and for believing in me. Love you, kiddo.

Jenni, Mitch and Chris, words cannot describe my love for you, and I am blessed that my marriage to Gary has brought you into my life.

Sport and Torey, who so lovingly slept on the bed and snored as I sat and typed, but always kept guard over me.

My parents—My mom, my dad and stepmom, who helped shape the events of my life and gave me plenty to learn about in life. Thank you for the sometimes hard, yet valuable, lessons you provided.

My sisters, Teresa and Sheila, who stood by me through happy and not-so-happy times. We have laughed, cried, sang, danced and prayed together and are the best of friends. Thank you for helping to pick up the pieces when life got really hard, love you.

My nieces and nephews, and RTJS2 and Gen, you have brought such joy, love and laughter to my life.

Mary Lou, thank you for your friendship and help with this book. Time to sing.

Leslie, you are my person, forever and always.

The Barbies, who are my tribe, words cannot express my love for these ladies and all we have been through together and will continue to do.

MiMi, thank you for being you and the gentle push, words of encouragement and prayers you always give me. Love and hugs.

Holly, thank you for the inspiration and sharing your peace, calm, laughter and love.

Deborah, thank you for the prayers, believing in me, helping me through the struggles, staying late and being with me until the end.

Dr. Gardner, thank you for the gentle and not-so-gentle push to become my true self.

Mrs. Palm, who taught me a lot about life, to believe in myself and work hard to accomplish things. Thank you.

Mikey, thank you for being you.

Thank you to Team Nickelson—y'all are the best.

A special thank you to the clients who have trusted me to help work through their emotions and learn to live their life and the many others who have been supportive of me during this process.

Thank you Lord for your guidance, love and presence. May I listen and hear your words and use them to help myself and others.

# ABOUT THE AUTHOR

Melissa lives in Fort Worth, Texas, and is a proud Texas girl. She lives with her husband, Gary, a family law attorney, her son, and two slightly spoiled dogs. Melissa was a family law legal assistant for 17 years before becoming a life coach and a Certified Divorce Coach. She has been divorced and knows firsthand the emotional roller coaster that follows. Melissa works with clients individually and in-group sessions to help others work through the pain, the emotional side of divorce. Melissa is fond of chocolate, shoe shopping, reading, traveling and exploring new places and is always up for a new adventure, especially if laughter is involved.
Her motto in life is: Choose Happy! Happiness is a choice.

Meet Melissa at www.MelissaNickelson.com

CPSIA information can be obtained
at www.ICGtesting.com
Printed in the USA
LVOW04s1513251016
510209LV00035B/541/P

9 780692 410639